JAGJIT ATWAL

A LIFE WELL LIVED

Sandeep Atwal

ISBN
Paperback 979-8-89961-081-3
Hardcase 979-8-89961-082-0

Made with ♥ on the Notion Press Platform

www.notionpress.com

Contents

CHAPTER 1

PROLOGUE

Jagjit had a great personality and endeared himself to everyone through his charm. He was near perfect in his professional knowledge, opinions, and deeds. He was proud of his manners and deeds. He was quite witty and loved to narrate from his repertoire of humorous jokes. Throughout his life, he faced many tragedies that gave him pain and suffering, but the strong person he was and ably supported by his wife Tejwant, he endured them with grace.

There were two events that had a profound influence on Jagjit's life. He was a family-loving person and was the eldest of his siblings, a sister Surinder, and a brother, Avtar. They were much younger than him, and "Veerji," as he was addressed by them, was looked up to by them for any guidance and support. Jagjit and his spouse, Tejwant, after their marriage, had taken on the responsibility for the care, education, and upbringing of Surinder and Avtar.

Surinder had been married to Jagjit Bhullar in 1963, and they were happily living together. At the time of their marriage, Jagjit Bhullar was employed as an Assistant Commandant in Punjab Armed Police and posted in Amritsar. I remember visiting them and the warm bonhomie that existed between Jagjit and his brother-in-law, Jagjit Bhullar. Kids soon followed – Sukhjit (alias Ashu) and, thereafter, Gurpreet (alias Minna). In the meanwhile, Jagjit Bhullar worked extremely hard and appeared for the competitive exams for the Punjab Civil Services and got selected as PCS Judicial. His initial assignment was as the Sub Divisional Magistrate at Samrala in Ludhiana District. They were a happy family, and we frequently visited them on weekends since it was a relatively short drive from Nangal, where Jagjit had been posted in the Bhakra Designs Directorate. It was just unexpected that we came to know of the sudden passing away of Jagjit Bhullar due to a heart attack while he was at home. This sudden, unfortunate development created an upheaval in the lives of Jagjit and Tejwant. Jagjit's only sister had become a widow at the early age of 35 and now had three kids (another girl child named Priya had been born by then) to look after. The responsibility of this young family came upon Jagjit, and he tried hard to shoulder it. Jagjit's father entrusted him with making all the decisions concerning Surinder and her young children. Late Jagjit Bhullar's friend, Rajbir Dhillon, came up with a proposal to marry Surinder. The condition was that she would only come along with the infant daughter Priya (later named as Pria), and that the boys Ashu and Minna would have to be taken care of by the two brothers, Jagjit and Avtar. This was a tough call since it involved breaking up the siblings and the subsequent effect on the boys who would have to grow up without their birth mother. Nevertheless, these calls were made, and Jagjit decided to take charge of Ashu and Avtar took the responsibility of Minna's upbringing. While Ashu joined Jagjit and Tejwant's household with their other three kids, since Avtar was still a bachelor, Minna was sent to Punjab Public School, Nabha, a boarding school. The sudden passing away of Jagjit Bhullar really imposed a big emotional and psychological burden on Jagjit.

Jagjit's brother Avtar was a police officer from the Indian Police Service (IPS) and was posted as the Deputy Inspector General of Jalandhar Range. He was physically located in Jalandhar and had the responsibility of the northern districts of the state of Punjab, including Amritsar. He operated out of his residence cum office and lived with his wife Amrita and son Harbir (Sunny). My wife, Linda, and I were visiting Chandigarh, where Jagjit was posted. It was Saturday, April

25, 1983, and we were all relaxing after a lovely breakfast when Jagjit got a call from one of his close friends. He informed Jagjit that while passing the Tribune office in Sector 30, the latest news signboard said, "DIG Atwal shot dead outside Golden Temple". We could see the color drain from Jagjit's face as he took in the news. After the confirmation from the Police Control Room, we all left for Jalandhar. This was a traumatic time for all of us, especially Jagjit and Tejwant, who had practically raised Avtar as their child. Upon reaching Jalandhar, Jagjit had to take charge of the situation since it was a huge emotional burden for Avtar's young widow, Amrita. The sudden and violent passing away of Avtar was a major turning point in Jagjit's life and shaped his further role.

CHAPTER 2

EARLY DAYS

The Atwal is a gotra (clan) within the Jat community, a large and diverse agricultural caste found in the northern regions of India, particularly in the states of Haryana, Punjab, Uttar Pradesh, and Rajasthan. The history of the Atwal clan is deeply rooted in the social and cultural fabric of the Jat community, and it is often associated with tales of valor, agricultural prowess, and community leadership. Like many other Jat clans, the Atwal clan has a rich oral tradition that recounts its members' lineage, achievements and struggles over the centuries. These stories often emphasize the Atwal clan's resilience, bravery, and contributions to the larger Jat community. It's important to note that the history and traditions of specific clans within the Jat community can vary based on regional and family-specific narratives. As such, the history of the Atwal clan may be recounted and celebrated in diverse ways by different members of the Jat community.

Atwals are one of the oldest Jat tribes, settling in the Punjab region during the Mahabharata era. They are mentioned in Sabha Parva of Mahabharata, Vayu Purana, and Markandeya Purana. There is unanimity among historians that Atwals used to husband camels, so they were originally known as the Oonth Wala, which changed over time first to Uthwal, then Athwal, and finally to Atwal. They mostly inhabited the Ambala, Ludhiana, Jalandhar, and Patiala districts of the Punjab, some settling as far west as Sialkot, Multan, Jhang, Montgomery, Muzaffargarh, and Bahawalpur in West Punjab,

4

in what is now Pakistan. After settling in West Punjab, many Atwal Jats converted to Islam, although most Atwals in India are Sikhs. Atwals are also found in large numbers in Amritsar and Gurdaspur. Some historians consider Atwals descendants of the Panwar and that they came to East Punjab from Multan. Jats, Khatris, Rajputs, and Dalits have a common background, and Atwal is a well-known and ancient sub-caste of Jats.

Jagjit's Ancestors

Our research indicates that the ancestral village of Jagjit was the Village Pharala, which is located about 15 km east of the Town of Phagwara. Phagwara has always been a major industrial town straddling the NH1 between Ludhiana and Jalandhar. Pharala was a small village overshadowed by its big cousin Behram, about 3 km to its south. Behram got its importance due to its location on the main Phagwara-Banga-Nawanshahr Road. Further, the populations of both these villages are almost identical with about 3500 residents per the 2001 census.

According to local tradition, Pharala was founded by Baba Hadal Atwal. Baba Hadal was married to a woman from Sandhwan. Since then, the village has also been known as "Sandhwan-Pharala". The villagers believe that Baba Hadal had three brothers. One moved and founded Chitti Pind (Jalandhar district), one moved and founded Khurad Pur (Jalandhar district), and the third moved and founded a village in Gurdaspur district known as "Athwal". Pharala has a historic **gurudwara** known as gurudwara Guru Har Rai Sahib Ji, named after Guru Har Rai, the seventh Sikh Guru who visited this place during his journey to Sri Anandpur Sahib during the Mughal era. The Atwal families who reside in or call home the Village Bir Puad (Kapurthala district) all hail from Pharala.

It is interesting to learn about the origin of the village Bir Puad (also known as Bir Pwahad). The original village of Pharala was in the floodplain of the river Bein and was subjected to frequent waterlogging, also called "Sem" in the local parlance. This river flows through about 400 villages and finally ends up as a tributary of the River Sutlej. The river Bein was also called Chitti (white) Bein, due to its clean waters, though of late it has been referred to as Kali (Black) Bein due to the high toxicity as lots of untreated effluents were discharged into it. There has been a concerted effort of late to clean up this river, and it is understood that the river is being restored to its earlier glory.

Back to the village of Pharala. Due to frequent waterlogging, over a period, the land became unfavorable for growing regular crops, and there was a need for the locals to seek arable land elsewhere. The families approached the Maharaja of Kapurthala since the revenue was being collected under his patronage. He told them to take the area of the "Bir" (the forest) that was adjacent to the village of Bhulla Rai located just due west of the town of Phagwara. Since most of the land was forested, it meant a lot of effort to clear it for farming and to settle a village. The seven brothers who took on this task were the pioneers and named the new settlement "Puad," and thus, over a period, it started getting named "Bir Puad." Since the early settlers were the seven brothers, all the residents of the Village Bir Puad can trace their bloodline and are related among themselves in some way or another.

Jagjit's grandfather, Waryam Singh, was originally a resident of Pharala and was among the seven brothers who were the first to settle in Bir Puad. Jagjit's father, Hari Singh (respectfully called Pitaji by his kids and Babaji by the grandkids), had a brother named Bikram Singh and a sister. There were two more minor brothers of Hari Singh who were unfortunately killed in a wall collapse while the family was still in Pharala. Hari Singh was really involved in the clearing of the forest in Bir Puad to make the land arable, create fields and water channels, dig wells, and construct houses for living. For this, he used to travel from Pharala regularly. At the same time, he was pursuing his studies at Phagwara and was one of the few who cleared the Matriculation examination. At that time, he was very well-versed in Urdu, Persian, Gurmukhi, and English. Since the official language for revenue purposes was Urdu, he joined the Revenue Department of the undivided Punjab as a junior revenue official. He was very hardworking and was posted at places like Karnal, Sirsa, Hissar, and Rohtak while finally retiring from Patti as a Zilledar. Hari Singh would have made a Tehsildar, but since the refugees who had come across from present-day Pakistan had to be accommodated in comparable positions, he made it to the position of a Zilledar only.

Hari Singh and Beant Kaur

Jagjit's Birth

Jagjit was born on December 7, 1929, at Chak 124, Village Shankar, near Lyallpur (now called Faisalabad, after King Faisal of Saudi Arabia). This is in present-day Pakistan. It was the place where his mother, Beant Kaur (affectionately called Bibiji), came from the family of the Takhar clan. The Takhars had large land holdings and were traditional farmers. It was a tradition that the expectant mother would relocate to her parents' house to deliver the newborn and then spend the next 40 days before joining her husband at his location. Jagjit's mother was the eldest of her siblings, of which there were five brothers and two sisters. Though not much is known about the family of Jagjit's mom's side, one sister was married to Harbhajan Singh of Village Bir Puad, but she passed away early. The entire family

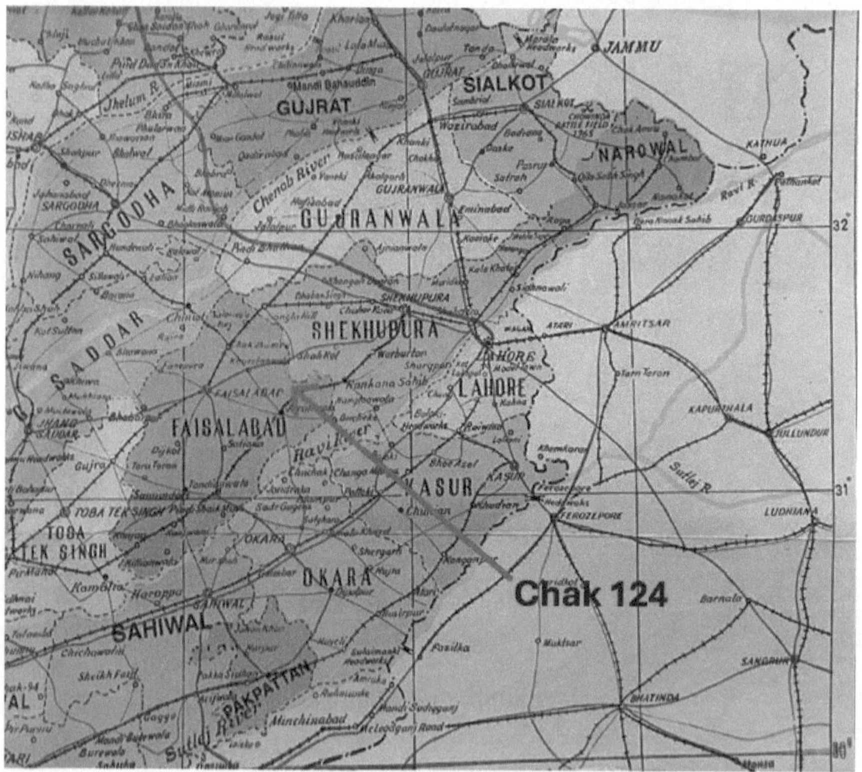

Birthplace of Jagjit

had relocated to India after partition and settled near Nakodar in the Jalandhar district, where land was allotted to them in villages Allowal and Dherian. Gurchetan, one of Bibiji's brothers, remained close to her. His daughter Varinder (also known as Shindi) got married to Makhan Singh, and they kept close touch with Jagjit's family. Makhan has since passed, and Shindi and her children are now settled in Sacramento, California.

Education

Jagjit did his studies at various Government schools where his father, Hari Singh, was posted. He completed his Vernacular Final and Middle School Examination in 1942 in the First Division while studying at the Government High School Sirsa, District Hissar of the undivided state of Punjab. Jagjit was an extremely hardworking and bright student with a passion for Mathematics. When Jagjit was about 12 years old, he almost lost his eyesight but soon recovered. The details that led to this are not completely known, but he had no lasting effect after this event. He passed his Matriculation examination in 1944 in the First Division while still at the Government High School, Sirsa. He passed the Intermediate Examination in Science in 1946 in the First Division while studying in the Government College, Rohtak. He was studying in Rohtak for his Bachelor of Arts (Hons in Mathematics) when the Partition of India took place. Jagjit was an exceptionally good student and excelled in academics. He was very athletic and fond of playing field hockey, where he was the Captain of the Government College, Rohtak team. Jagjit graduated at the top of his class in First Division for the final examination in 1949. It was due to this academic achievement and his excellence in sports that he was admitted to the University of Roorkee (Then known as the Punjab University Faculty of Engineering and Technology). He also got a scholarship for this program, which was an immense help since the tuition and the hostel fees were steep, which his father could

Registered No. 48,ir.582.   Roll No.   3615.

EAST PANJAB UNIVERSITY

FACULTY OF ARTS

SESSION 1948.

This is to certify that

Jagjit Singh   son ~~daughter~~ of

S. Hari Singh   and of the

Government College, Rohtak   has obtained the Degree of

Bachelor of Arts

with Honours in   Mathematics,   in this University on the result of

the Examination held in   September , 1948, in which he/~~she~~ was placed

in the   First   Division.

Passed the Examination ~~xxxxxxx~~/as a whole.

Passed also in Military Science   Additional Optional Subject

Countersigned

SOLAN (Simla Hills)

March 5, 1949.   Chancellor   Registrar

Jagjit BA (Hons) Degree

Roll No. 8

Panjab University

FACULTY OF ENGINEERING & TECHNOLOGY

This is to certify

That _Jagjit Singh Atwal_, Regd. No. _48.ir.582_,

son of _Shri Hari Singh Atwal_, and of

the _Punjab Engineering College, Roorkee_, has

been admitted to the Degree of

Bachelor of Science in Engineering (Civil)

in this University having passed the Examination held

in _June_, _1952_, in the _First_ Division.

Countersigned

SOLAN (*Simla Hills*),

December 4, *1954*.

Chancellor

Registrar

Jagjit Engineering Degree 1954

11

hardly afford. Roorkee University was very well-known for its civil engineering program, and Jagjit pursued it while he was there.

Partition 1947

The Partition of India in August 1947 triggered a large-scale demographic upheaval which led to the displacement of millions of people from their living places. Along with other central districts of the united Punjab, the Ambala division also experienced riots and devastation during those critical months of partition in 1947. Gurgaon, Rohtak, Simla, and many other areas of this division experienced communal bloodbaths. The authorities had to impose special regulations to curb the violence, which was on communal lines. At Gurgaon, the roads of many villages and towns were littered here and there with dead bodies. Lots of houses were burned down. Nature also turned destructive and showed its worst side. The monsoon of 1947 was unparalleled in its fierceness and for its unusually longer duration. The rains came on with fury and played havoc with the marching caravans and flooded the roads and bridges.

The Atwal family was at Rohtak in the undivided Punjab at that time. Jagjit had completed his Matriculation and had gone to Lahore for an interview for his undergraduate program when the preparations for the partition took place. He returned to Rohtak well in time to escape the unfortunate happenings of that time. The family residence was in the predominantly Muslim areas of Rohtak. Though the relations with the neighbors had been cordial earlier, they started getting strained because of the happenings among the communities. It was a well-known fact that Hari Singh had a 12-bore shotgun and a sword, which he had acquired during his duty some time ago. Since Hari Singh had very uncertain work timings, he used to leave early and get back late to avoid confrontations with the crowds who were looking for revenge for the killings of their relatives in other parts of the country. It was quite common for Muslims to pick up young girls and take them away. Jagjit's sister Surinder was only seven at that time.

One day, many Muslim neighbors gathered outside the Atwal residence, looking for trouble. Jagjit's mother, Beant Kaur, went outside and told them that her husband was inside waiting for them with his gun and sword, whereas in fact, he was not even home. After some discussions among them, the crowd decided to disperse, and a calamity was averted. Jagjit was a good sportsman and used to play hockey at his college. Since he used to return late after practice, it was a cause of worry for the family in those uncertain times. Jagjit also joined the team at the Rohtak Refugee Camp to help with the other families in the community. This was a very well-organized camp, and supplies for the residents were brought from Delhi and then distributed. Volunteering at this camp was a wonderful way to give back to the community who had been displaced from their ancestral lands in the newly created nation of Pakistan. It was also during this time that his infant sister suffered an unfortunate and premature death due to accidentally swallowing a bar of soap.

Roorkee

Roorkee College was established in 1847 by James Thomson, the Lieutenant Governor of the North-Western Provinces. This was the first engineering college in the British Empire on the Indian subcontinent. The college was renamed as Thomson College of Civil Engineering in 1854. In Punjab, a College of Engineering was established at Lahore in 1921 and named as Punjab Engineering College. After the Partition of India in 1947, this was relocated to the Roorkee campus of the Thomson College of Engineering. It was given the status of a University by Act No. IX of 1948 of U.P., Govt. in recognition of its performance and potential and considering the needs of post-independent India. Pt. Jawaharlal Nehru, the first Prime Minister of India, presented the Charter in November 1949 elevating the erstwhile college to the first engineering University of independent India. Since Roorkee was the only well-known engineering college in North India during that time, it was the dream of all aspiring engineers to study at that institution and it was a matter of honor to be selected and granted admission to this prestigious institution of learning. Jagjit had his mind made to study civil engineering and become an engineer. Funds were scarce, and his father could not afford the tuition and lodging. However, since Jagjit was an exceptionally good student and had stood first in his college and secured exceptionally good marks in his Bachelor of Arts program with Honors in Mathematics, he was accepted at Roorkee and granted a scholarship. This enabled Jagjit to pursue his dream and finish his Civil Engineering degree.

After joining the Punjab Engineering College at Roorkee, Jagjit quickly immersed himself in the routine and pursued his love of sports, particularly hockey. He was on the college hockey team and excelled in cricket and swimming. He developed a fine swimming style, enabling him to pass on the teaching to his children later in life. Upon completion of his degree, Jagjit went on to do an internship at Tohana for 5 months prior to joining the Irrigation Department of Punjab in 1952. Jagjit became friends with some fine individuals he was attached to throughout his life. Most of these friends and colleagues joined the Punjab Irrigation Department, which was rapidly hiring qualified engineers to construct hydel dams, irrigation networks, and power plants downstream of these projects. I vividly remember Jagjit taking us to Roorkee to visit his alma mater much later in life. We were young, and I was around 10 years old, but I still recall the excitement in his step as we toured the campus. Much had changed, but he was nostalgic as we went around the hostels, mess, classrooms, sports facilities, and the café, where they made some heavenly tea biscuits. I had an opportunity to visit the campus by myself much later as an adult, but it did not have such an impact compared to my previous visit with my father. Roorkee itself is a small town with a cantonment, but the University has been and still is its main attraction. Situated along a wide canal, it provides rowing facilities as well.

From where Jagjit had graduated, the Punjab Engineering College at Roorkee was moved to its present location at the new city of Chandigarh. This was done due to the division of Punjab into present-day Punjab and Haryana on November 1st, 1966, while the hilly areas were merged with the state of Himachal Pradesh. The erstwhile Roorkee University has since been upgraded to an Indian Institute of Technology. However, the original buildings still exude the grandeur which had the original layout established by the British.

CHAPTER 3

JAGJIT BEGINS HIS CAREER

Bhakra Dam

Nestled amidst the Shivalik Hills in Himachal Pradesh, the Bhakra Dam is an enduring symbol of India's post-independence ambition and engineering prowess. Towering at a height of 226 meters this straight gravity dam on the Sutlej River is a marvel of design and a lifeline for millions across North India. Its story is one of vision, resilience, and transformation—a tale that intertwines the hopes of a young nation with the realities of modern development.

The Bhakra Dam, which was conceptualized by the British as early as 1910, kept getting revised in scope and cost, but the basic plans of the location and the design essentially remained the same. However, it was after independence that the project took definitive shape. In 1948, under the guidance of the then Prime Minister Jawaharlal Nehru, the Bhakra-Nangal Project was inaugurated, marking the dawn of a new era for India's infrastructure development. Built over the next fifteen years, the dam was completed in 1963, with the help of engineers, workers, and planners who overcame immense challenges, including difficult terrain and the lack of advanced machinery. Nehru famously referred to the dam as "The Temple of Resurgent India," highlighting its symbolic significance in nation-building.

The Bhakra Dam is one of the highest gravity dams in the world, designed to withstand colossal water pressure. Its reservoir, Gobind Sagar, is a sprawling 168-square-kilometer expanse that can hold up to 9.34 billion cubic meters of water. The dam's powerhouses generate a substantial 1,325 megawatts of hydroelectric power, making it a cornerstone of India's energy infrastructure. The complex also includes the downstream Nangal Dam, which regulates water flow and supplies the irrigation channels. Together, the Bhakra-Nangal duo has revolutionized agriculture and energy in the region.

Before Bhakra Dam, Punjab and Haryana heavily depended on unpredictable monsoon rains for agriculture. The dam's extensive canal system transformed this scenario, enabling year-round irrigation for over ten million hectares of farmland. This irrigation network played a pivotal role in India's Green Revolution of the 1960s and 1970s, which catapulted the country to self-sufficiency in food production. Crops like wheat and rice flourished, turning Punjab into the "Granary of India." Farmers' lives were transformed, and rural economies experienced a significant boost.

Beyond irrigation, the Bhakra Dam complex contributes significantly to India's energy grid. The hydroelectric power generated here supports industrial and domestic consumption across multiple states, including Punjab, Haryana, Rajasthan, and Himachal

Pradesh. As a renewable energy source, it reduces dependency on fossil fuels, aligning with global sustainability goals.

Jagjit's involvement in the design and construction of this massive project was significant. The collapse of the penstock during the construction of the Bhakra Dam occurred on November 16, 1959, and was a significant event in the project's history. The incident occurred during the installation of one of the large penstocks designed to carry water from the reservoir to the turbines in the powerhouse.

The primary cause of the penstock collapse was structural failure related to the improper installation of the penstock sections. Specifically, the collapse occurred when a welded joint in the penstock, which was part of the complex piping system, failed under pressure. This failure was exacerbated by poor alignment, excessive internal water pressure, and inadequate stress distribution at the welded joints. The installation procedure was not as rigorous as needed for such a high-stress component, contributing to the eventual breakdown.

The collapse of the penstock resulted in a major setback to the construction schedule, causing both material damage and time loss. It also led to further investigations into design flaws and the methods used for installing critical components of the dam's infrastructure.

The incident prompted changes in construction techniques and reinforced the need for more stringent quality control and testing in assembling such high-stress structures. Engineers at the time analyzed the failure thoroughly, and lessons learned from this event contributed to improvements in dam engineering practices, particularly in the design and installation of penstocks and other vital infrastructure components.

Bhakra Design Office

Sited in the Bhakra Gorge on the Sutlej River, the highest straight gravity dam of the world at that time was planned to look after the growing demand for irrigation and power for the area of Punjab, PEPSU (Patiala and Eastern Punjab States Union), and Rajasthan. It would be pertinent to note that the state of Punjab of that era included the now states of Haryana and Himachal Pradesh. PEPSU was subsequently amalgamated with the state of Punjab in 1956. Since the entire project was being funded by the Central Government and the workforce provided by the state of Punjab, this was a joint effort, and a few American consultants were also hired to provide the necessary technical advice.

The original office of the Bhakra Design Directorate was established in the growing city of New Delhi in early 1950. The city of New Delhi was itself being constructed rapidly to house Government Offices and residential houses for the staff. The first Bhakra Design Directorate was established near the vacant grounds of the present-day Supreme Court. Though initially some space was allotted in the Central Power and Water Commission (CPWC) building for their offices, the entire staff lived in tents. Gradually, the offices were also moved to the same location. As more accommodation became available, the staff moved to the houses in newly built Kaka Nagar.

Jagjit joined the Design Directorate as an Assistant Design Engineer (ADE) in 1952 after completion of his internship at Tohana, which is currently in Haryana. His family had since moved to Patti in Amritsar district on his father's posting to that location. Since most of the new hires were all recent engineering graduates from Roorkee University, they knew each other well, and almost all of them were bachelors. The staff quarters at Kaka Nagar had been planned and constructed as family accommodation; thus, the single officers shared a house. Jagjit shared a house with his good friend M.N. Sharma, and they had engaged a cook and caretaker for this house.

Working daily with the Design Directorate from the tented accommodation became exceedingly difficult. The summer and winter seasons made for their challenges, and the dust proved to be a big problem for the maintenance and storage of the designs of the various aspects of the Bhakra Dam as it kept getting built at the site in Punjab. Therefore, it was decided that the Design Directorate be moved to some residential houses in Kaka Nagar itself. This solved the problem of the storage and dustproofing of the valuable designs.

Bhakra Dam Presentation

CHAPTER 4

JAGJIT STARTS A FAMILY

Atma Singh

Prior to going into the marriage of Jagjit and Tejwant, it would be appropriate to share some relevant details about Tejwant and the illustrious and educated family she came from. Tejwant's parents, Atma Singh Berar (affectionately called Papaji) and Amrit Berar (affectionately called Beji), came from modest backgrounds in villages in Punjab. Tejwant's grandfather, Bachan Singh, was born in the Ganji Gulab Singh Wala village near Bagha Purana in Punjab. After passing Matriculation from Malwa Khalsa High School in Ludhiana, he joined Roorkee College of Engineering, which at that time only offered a two-year Diploma in engineering. After completing his Diploma, he joined the Uttar Pradesh Irrigation department as an Overseer in Etawah, where he supervised the construction of irrigation canals. Due to his hard work and dedication, he was selected to work at the Port of Basra in Iraq, where he oversaw canal construction. Upon his return to U.P., he was promoted to Sub Divisional Officer and was posted in various locations. After retirement, he established a girls' school in Rode village near Moga.

Bachan Singh had four sons, Santokh Singh, Atma Singh, Gurdial Singh and Iqbal Singh. Santokh Singh passed his Matriculation from Malwa Khalsa High School, Ludhiana and B.Sc. from Khalsa College, Amritsar. He joined B.Sc. in engineering at the University of Michigan at Ann Arbor, Illinois in the USA. Sardar Partap Singh Kairon (later Chief Minister of Punjab) was also at the same University at the same time for M.A. in Political Science. After completing their respective

Degrees, they returned to India in 1929. Due to the Great Depression of 1929, they could not find any job as there were very few opportunities and they joined the Shiromani Gurdwara Parbandhak Committee (S.G.P.C.) at Amritsar. As the Secretary of S.G.P.C., Santokh Singh brought several improvements in the management of Sri Harmandir Sahib. He got the Guru Ram Das Sarai constructed, which had 250 rooms for the stay of outstation devotees. At that time, the Prashad was prepared by shops outside the Gurdwara. He started the preparation of the Prashad inside the Golden Temple complex for distribution, a practice that has continued since. A few years later, Santokh Singh got a job in the Punjab Irrigation Department and was posted in various locations in the undivided India (present-day Pakistan).

His family was well settled there, but the Partition of India in 1947 was not a good thing for them. At that time, he was posted at Valeri near Multan as an Executive Engineer (XEN). Their eldest son, Avtar Singh had been spending the summer vacations with his uncle, Atma Singh and his family in Simla when the announcement of the Partition of India was made. Avtar Singh's family, comprising of his parents, three brothers and a sister, were ambushed at Pakpattan while they were driving to cross the newly created border, and they all lost their lives. Eventually, Atma Singh and Amrit Kaur took up the responsibility of the 15-year-old Avtar Singh, who became part of their large family.

Atma Singh was born in 1912 in Achhalda near Etawah in Uttar Pradesh. He was the next in line and worked hard to complete his BSc from Allahabad University. Eventually, he joined the Indian Revenue Service, where he rose over a period to become a Deputy Director of Central Excise and Customs – Ex-officio Deputy Secretary, Revenue Department, Government of India. The next brother, Gurdial Singh, also studied and completed his graduation. He went on to get married to Raj Kumari (Lalli) Mangat and set up a successful furniture business named Model Furnishers at Darya Ganj, Delhi. The youngest brother, Iqbal Singh, was the most handsome. He was studying for his graduation in Economics in Lucknow when he contracted chickenpox, which proved to be fatal.

Amrit Kaur

Amrit Kaur was born in 1916 and came from a family of Dhaliwals. They belonged to the village of Lopon in the Moga district. The marriage union between Atma Singh and Amrit Kaur was arranged when they were very young. Atma Singh insisted that his wife Amrit's family ensure she was educated. Toward this, Amrit Kaur was sent to the residence school at Sidhwan Bet, and she spent two years there toward formal education. This held them in good stead

Atma Singh and Amrit Kaur

later as they could exchange letters and make decisions while being separated due to the frequent moves which came about as part of Atma Singh's job. The formal marriage took place in 1933, and it was around the same time that Atma Singh had been gainfully employed as Superintendent Central Excise and Customs and had the means to look after his family and provide for them. It was an unwritten rule that the women in those days were homemakers.

Atma Singh and Amrit Kaur had several postings and traveled to many parts of India. They had seven children, and the frequent transfers meant that the education of their children was not regular since they changed schools often while moving between Rajasthan, (undivided) Punjab, Uttar Pradesh, Gujarat, and Bengal. The four sisters and three brothers were closely knit, and they helped their parents by sharing responsibilities and chores. Satwant (Lily) was the eldest, Tejwant (Tej, Kamal), Ravinder (Baby), Jogeshwar (Jogi), Bhopinder (Bhopi), Hrideshwar (Kuku), and finally Harinder (Billoo) followed in that sequence.

Matchmaking for Jagjit

Atma Singh was posted at Alwar, Rajasthan in 1954. Lily and Tej were visiting their uncle Gurdial Singh and their aunt Lalli in Delhi for the summer vacation. Gurdial Singh informed them that some people would be coming over without giving any indication of what it was all about. The people in question were Jagjit's mother, Beant Kaur, his sister, Surinder, and his brother, Avtar. Over lunch, some polite conversations took place, and the sisters (Lily and Tej) had no idea what it was all about. The visit over, it was all forgotten and the sisters returned to Alwar. Meanwhile, Atma Singh had moved to Cooch Behar in Bengal on a transfer, while the family stayed back at Alwar for the children to complete the school year. In early 1955, Tej's father wrote to her that Jagjit's family, who had come to meet them in Delhi the previous summer, had proposed a marriage between Jagjit and Tej. It was also revealed that initially the visit by Jagjit's family was supposed to meet Lily as the prospective bride, but Tej was chosen instead.

To put it in context, the whole matchmaking process began when Jagjit had made a visit to Model Furnishers, the business owned by Gurdial Singh in early 1954. Jagjit had been allotted a house in Kaka Nagar on a sharing basis, and he needed some furniture. Over the course of discussions, Gurdial Singh and Jagjit became friends, and Jagjit was invited to visit Gurdial Singh's residence, which happened to be right above the showroom in Darya Ganj. Gurdial Singh took a liking to Jagjit and enquired about his background and family. Throughout various meetings, Gurdial Singh introduced Jagjit to various organizations like the Lions Club, Jat Sikh Association, National Sports Club of India (NSCI), etc. The NSCI was close to where Jagjit resided and had a competition-sized swimming pool which Jagjit used regularly thereafter.

In April 1955, Tej and her siblings went to Cooch Behar to visit their father, who had been posted there the previous year. The formalities of the marriage alliance had not taken place, though it was assumed that the wedding would be formalized at the right time. Tej was sent to Maharani college Jaipur to reside in the hostel and undergo the Bachelor of Arts program there. Jogi also accompanied her to complete his graduation from the Maharaja College, which incidentally was located just across the road. Shortly thereafter, the formal engagement (Shagan) took place between Jagjit and Tej, and all study plans took a back seat. Tej did complete her F.A. (First Year of Arts).

Shagan

The summer of 1956 saw Atma Singh posted to Meerut, and the family moved there too. In the meantime, Hari Singh also moved from Rohtak to Patti in Amritsar district during that period. It was the family of the bride that used to take the "Shagan" to the family of the groom. The "Shagan" symbolized that the family of the bride was interested in the groom and offered some gifts to him to sort of "commit" him to the upcoming marriage. This was the practice followed for all arranged marriages. There was no occasion for the prospective groom and bride to meet prior to their marriage. However, this process was short-circuited a bit in the case of Jagjit and Tej. Since Gurdial Singh had introduced Jagjit to NSCI and was aware that Jagjit used to frequent the pool, Gurdial Singh's wife Lalli's brother Harnam and sister Seebo insisted that this provided an opportunity for Tej to see her prospective husband for the first time. Toward this, they took Tej along with them to the NSCI poolside restaurant and ordered some tea. When Jagjit came there, Tej had her first glimpse of Jagjit in his swimming trunks! As she affectionately recalled later, she was disappointed at first sight. As the formal engagement had taken place between them and Jagjit was quite friendly with Gurdial Singh and his family, this allowed Tej and Jagjit to meet there.

It was not until almost three years before he decided to get married - all because his colleague and roommate, M.N. Sharma, who was an amateur astrologer, told him that since he was a Manglik, he had to stay single until he was twenty-seven. Anyway, it was all for the good since the marriage that took place on December 07, 1956 - incidentally, the day he turned 27 - had stood rock solid for over 59 years. In hindsight, I guess the Manglik prediction was pretty accurate.

The Wedding

Friday the 7th of December 1956 was chosen as the date for the wedding of Jagjit and Tej. As was the custom, the wedding party (The Baraat) used to travel from the house of the groom to the location of the bride's residence. Since this involved a fair bit of travel from Patti in Punjab to Meerut in Uttar Pradesh, only the male members of the groom's family traveled for the actual wedding. Jagjit's family members arrived at Meerut by train on the 6th of December. Lodging arrangements were made, and the actual wedding took place the next day.

The weddings used to be a simple affair and were normally conducted at the residence of the bride where the Akhand Path was conducted. The Akhand Path is the continuous non-stop recitation of all the verses of the Shri Guru Granth Sahib from the beginning to the end in 31 Ragas, in all 1430 pages and normally lasts 48 hours by a team of readers. The culmination of the Akhand Path led into the Anand Karaj, which is the actual wedding ceremony, in the presence of the family and friends.

Hari Singh and Atma Singh

The Anand Karaj is the Sikh marriage ceremony, meaning "Act toward happiness" or "Act toward a happy life", was introduced by Guru Amar Das. The four *laavaan* (hymns which take place during the ceremony) were composed by his successor, Guru Ram Das, and are recited and sung to solemnize the nuptials. Although the recitation of the *laavaan* in Sikh ceremonies is a historical and enduring tradition, the practice of circumambulating around the Guru Granth Sahib to conduct a marriage ceremony is a relatively recent innovation that supplanted the tradition of circumambulating around the sacred fire (havan) in the early twentieth century. The groom and the bride take four rounds around the Guru Granth Sahib in a clockwise direction while the *Raagis* (singers) recite the *laavaan*. Prior to the commencement of the *laavaan*, the father of the bride hands over the edge of the bride's garment (pallu) into the hands of the groom, signifying the passing on of the responsibility of the bride to her would be husband who would now support and protect her henceforth.

Wedding Pictures

After the wedding and traditional vegetarian lunch, the wedding party departed the same evening and went back to Patti via Amritsar. This was preceded by the "Doli," which is a traditional send-off by the family of the bride. Since many members of the wedding party had come from the now-ancestral village of Bir Puad, they got off the train en route at Phagwara. There are few pictures of the wedding, but it is fair to say that the relevant one available does capture the attendance. It was also a tradition from the bride's family to give some relevant household items to the newly married couple to assist them in starting a new household. However, since Jagjit was very forward-thinking and not a traditional person, he was not in favor of this. Nevertheless, some items did find their way to Patti. After spending a couple of days at her in-law's house at Patti, Tej and Jagjit returned to Delhi on December 12th to the residence that he shared with his good friend M.N. Sharma. Tej enjoyed the fuss made by the cook and housekeeper, who had been employed by Jagjit previously.

New Delhi

After about two weeks of this arrangement, Jagjit applied for separate accommodation and was allotted a house in nearby Shan Nagar (now known as Bharti Nagar). This was a bigger place, and two families shared the accommodation. Since Jagjit's siblings loved their "Veerji," Jagjit and Tej went back to Patti for the Christmas holidays. It was probably around the same time that I was conceived! It was a happy time for the young couple, and they really explored the vistas of the capital city of New Delhi on bicycle and public transport. Lodhi Gardens was just across the road from their residence, and they frequented it, as well as the famous Khan Market, now an iconic shopping complex. Khan Market was also an easy transport hub to get buses to travel to various parts of the city. Jagjit used to take his bicycle to work at Kaka Nagar, about 2 km away. He used to make it a point to come for lunch with his new bride.

New Delhi 1956

Jagjit had a good friend named Badri Narayan Mehra. He was an insurance broker but also a keen photographer and had his own equipment for processing photographs. He had taken some nice photographs of Tej in and around the Lodhi Gardens, with one showing off the baby bump, too! Another of Jagjit's good friends was Vinay Kumar, who resided in the nearby colony of Golf Links. Vinay was Jagjit's junior in Roorkee, and they had continued their association since.

Jagjit's siblings, Surinder and Avtar, came to stay with them for the summer of 1957. They traveled by train from Patti and enjoyed staying in the big city even though the summer heat did not permit them to explore it fully. They went to various historical landmarks and even visited Qutub Minar, which was a bit out of the city. It was during that visit that Surinder lost a gold earring that she had borrowed from Tej. Avtar was upset with her carelessness, but this was soon forgotten with the bonhomie that the siblings enjoyed.

Tej used to go to Willingdon Hospital (now called Lok Nayak Jai Prakash Hospital) for routine follow-ups while pregnant with her first child. After one visit, she decided to quickly visit and meet the family of one of Papaji's friends, Sohan Singh, who used to live at Gole Market, which was adjacent to the hospital. Time passed and Tej did not realize she had overstayed, and Jagjit really started worrying for her safety. Jagjit contacted Tej's uncle, Gurdial Singh, and they started looking for her on Gurdial Singh's motorcycle. It was a big relief when Tej was located at Sohan Singh's residence, but it was surely a scary time for them.

September 27, 1957, was a joyful day for Jagjit and Tej when their first child was born. A son, Sandeep, came into their lives, and their life was not the same again. Jagjit's mother, Beant Kaur, had come from Patti to live with them and help for the delivery and subsequent recuperation. She stayed almost a month and was a tremendous help. Since Sandeep was the first child to be born on both sides of the family, he was lucky to be loved by all.

CHAPTER 5

Jagjit's Family Responsibility

As alluded to earlier, Jagjit's father Hari Singh, though he had a stable job, did not pay well enough for him to afford the education of all his children. He had ensured that Jagjit was admitted for his engineering degree, though scholarships were the main reason he could graduate and get a stable government job. It had been made succinctly clear to Jagjit that henceforth, the responsibility of the education of his siblings, Surinder and Avtar, would be his. Despite the expenses of a growing family and living in a relatively expensive metropolis of New Delhi, Jagjit and Tej got Surinder admitted to the Intermediate program of the Kanya Mahavidyalaya, a college for women in Jalandhar. She joined the hostel, and Jagjit and Tej borne the fees for board and lodging plus tuition.

Avtar completed his Matriculation from Phagwara in 1960 and came to Delhi to live with Jagjit and Tej. It was around the same time when Jagjit and Tej welcomed their second child into their family. Manoj, their second son, was born in the Holy Family Hospital on January 11, 1960. The delivery was normal again, and since Papaji had now been posted in New Delhi and stayed at Paharganj, there was sufficient family support to assist them for the arrival of their second child. Tej's siblings were very loving to her children, and it really helped that they all lived close. Jagjit was now allotted a bigger house in Kaka Nagar, which was comfortable.

Avtar did very well in his Matriculation from Phagwara, and based on his good marks, he was admitted to the Prep program at

Hindu College. Unfortunately, his academic level was much higher in Delhi, and despite trying his best, Avtar did not do well on the final exam. This really jolted him, and it became a challenge for him to get admission in any college for the bachelor's program. After trying many avenues, Avtar finally got admission to Khalsa College. Avtar got serious about his studies and devoted his time to the completion of his Bachelor of Arts program. Since there was a lot of responsibility for the education of his siblings, Jagjit and Tej diverted most of his salary toward that. He did not enjoy any holidays or vacations during this period.

5th Wedding Anniversary

Jagjit and Tej welcomed their third child, a girl whom they named Juhi, on October 3rd, 1962, born at the Lady Irwin Hospital. Papaji had now moved to the multistoried flats at Kidwai Nagar. With an expanding family, Jagjit needed independent transportation and got a Rajdoot motorcycle. This enabled the family to go around the city easily without getting tied to public transportation. This motorcycle really proved to be very helpful for the family moving around and not limited to public transport. However, since the family comprised of three kids now, this could be problematic at times. During a trip to Connaught Place, the traffic police stopped Jagjit since he had the entire family on the motorcycle. After being let off with a warning, which brought an end to the family trips on the motorcycle.

Avtar

The aggression by the Chinese started in the eastern part of India in 1962. The Indian armed forces did not have the necessary forces to provide a strong resistance, and there was widespread concern of a major debacle. Fortunately for India, the Chinese incursion stopped as suddenly as it had started, but it did reveal some real shortcomings in the strength of the Indian armed forces. A major decision was taken to provide for an Emergency Commission in the officer cadre of the three services. Avtar was still in the bachelor's program and keen to join. Jagjit insisted that Avtar finish the remaining part of the graduation and then look to join the armed forces if he still had the interest.

Avtar graduated with good marks and applied for and got selected in the officer cadre of the Indian Army in the EC-7 course. He was allotted the Artillery arm and, after the required training, was posted to the YOL Camp in (now) Himachal Pradesh. The location YOL (Young Officers Living) was established around 1849 close to the town of Dharamsala, and the cantonment came up in 1942. The camp was famously used by the British to house the German POWs after the First World War and then the Italian POWs after the Second World War.

Avtar's unit was in Jalandhar Cantonment just before the 1965 war with Pakistan. Though this Artillery unit did not see actual action on the front line, they were held in reserve for any eventualities. Fortunately, the actual conflict lasted a short time before the ceasefire was declared. The aggressive posturing between the two countries was withdrawn, and the offensive forces returned to their peacetime locations. Avtar had not been made for a life in the Army with its regimented lifestyle. When there was a disbandment of the Emergency Commission officers, Avtar was among the majority who were let go. His father, Hari Singh, did not take this news very kindly, and Avtar started considering his options. Avtar was a very diligent individual, and once he made up his mind for something, he went headlong into it to achieve it. On the advice of Atma Singh, father of Tejwant, he decided to appear for the Civil Services examination, and as a buildup for it, he moved in with his parents at the village. This provided for an uninterrupted preparation for this tough competitive examination. Avtar managed to pass the Prelims and then did very well in the interview stage, too. Even though he aimed to join the Indian Administrative Services (IAS), his merit permitted him to make the list for the Indian Police Services (IPS). He was determined to make it for the IAS in the next attempt the following year.

After a full year of very concentrated studies and preparation, Avtar did improve his position, but it still was not enough to make it to the IAS, as the competition was strong. Avtar joined the IPS and went to the National Police Academy at Mount Abu, Rajasthan for training where he found many of his friends and colleagues from the Army days. After the one-year training at the Police Academy, Avtar came up high in merit and was allotted his preferred home state of Punjab. His first posting was an Assistant Superintendent of

Police (ASP) at Gurdaspur. His grooming in the Army did assist him in settling down into another profile of law enforcement. During this period, the war with Pakistan happened in the winter of 1971. We did visit him at Gurdaspur after the ceasefire and had the privilege of seeing the "Patton Graveyard," where many destroyed Pakistani tanks were put together. We even got an opportunity to go into Pakistan territory, which was still occupied by the Indian ground forces. I distinctly remember going into the Kot Naina Police Station, which was remarkably intact and was serving as an impromptu office of the local Indian military officers. Shortly thereafter, he was posted as the Commandant of the Police Recruits Training College (PRTC) at Jahan Khelan. We had a wonderful experience visiting him and seeing the various training activities there.

In early 1973, he was deputed to the BSF as the Commandant of a Battalion at Fazilka. At this time, he got engaged and married Amrita Randhawa, who belonged to a well-known family from the village of Ramdass in the Amritsar District. I had passed my written examination for the UPSC for admission to the National Defense Academy and was scheduled to be called up for the Services Selection Board. Avtar advised me to come to his location and conduct preparation for the interview stage. It was a wonderful few weeks that I spent with him among the BSF troops who had set up an obstacle course for me to practice, and I also had the opportunity to undertake some horse-riding lessons. The dates for the interview for the Air Force Selection Board at Clement Town, Dehra Doon, clashed with the marriage dates for Avtar's wedding, and I missed all the festivities. The bright thing that came out from here was that I made it through the interview and medical and was selected to be part of the Air Force stream of the NDA and joined the 52nd course in Khadakwasla in July 1974.

After his wedding, Avtar got posted as Superintendent of Police at Amritsar and settled into married life. Amrita and he welcomed their only child, a son they named Harbir, affectionately called Sunny. The family bonds were remarkably close, and they spent many happy moments together. Promotions followed, and he moved to Chandigarh in the CID Department for a while and thereafter to Patiala as the Senior Superintendent of Police. He was very well-liked by his colleagues, subordinates, and seniors. He was one of the most junior officers to have made it to the rank of Deputy Inspector General of Police and was given charge of the Jalandhar Range. In this position of responsibility, he undertook the visit to the Golden Temple at Amritsar on April 25, 1983. Being in civilian clothes, he paid obeisance at the holy shrine, and as he was exiting the complex, he was assassinated and paid the ultimate sacrifice. For his devotion to duty, he was posthumously awarded the Police Medal of Honor.

Avtar Singh Atwal

The entire administration and police fraternity rallied around the family, and Amrita was inducted into the Punjab Civil Services, where she spent time in various roles until her secondment to the Indian Administrative Services before her retirement. Their son, Harbir, graduated from Law School and was then selected to the Punjab Police Academy, Phillaur, where he graduated at the top of his class and was awarded the Sword of Honor. He continues to serve in the Punjab Police and is currently the Superintendent of Police at Mohali. He lives with his mother, Amrita, his wife, Aman, and their son, Sumer, in Chandigarh.

DIG shot dead outside Golden Temple

Injured boy dies in hospital

Express News Service
AMRITSAR, April 23.
Mr A. S. Atwal, Deputy Inspector-General of Police (DIG), Jullundur range, was shot dead by an unidentified youth outside the main entrance of the Golden Temple on Monday.

A schoolboy, Bikramjit Singh, who was also hit by gun-shots, died in the emergency ward of Guru Teg Bahadur hospital. Mr Kulwinder Singh, of the Central Reserve Police Force (CRPF), the third person injured in the outburst of gun-shots, is lying in a precarious condition in the same hospital.

The assailant, a young man of medium height, after firing the shots from a carbine, entered the Golden Temple, the Senior Superintendent of Police (SSP), Mr Surjit Singh Bains, told PNS in the city Kotwali later in the afternoon.

The incident took place at 11.20 a.m.

Mr Atwal, 40, had gone to the Golden Temple around 10 a.m. After visiting the temple as the DIG turned left at the main entrance, the assailant opened fire. The schoolboy and the CRPF man were also visiting the Golden Temple.

The schoolboy was with his mother and grand-parents and the CRPF man, belonging to a nearby village, was accompanying his family.

The SSP said that the assailant opened fire at the DIG from a very close range.

The deputy commissioner, Mr Sardar Singh, and Mr Bains and other senior police officers, including Mr J. P. Birdi, SP, head quarters, immediately reached the spot. Mr Lehna Singh Tur, the Akali Dal Lok Sabha member, also accompanied government and the police officers.

Mr Atwal was in plain clothes. He was hit by six to seven shots in the head and arms and died on the spot.

Mr Kulwinder Singh, 30, is reportedly on leave and came to the Golden Temple for prayers. He is posted in Goa.

Mr Atwal was among the police officials present when the militant Sikh leader, Jarnail Singh Bhindranwale, courted arrest in Amritsar in September 1981.

An ex-Army captain, Mr Atwal was said to have been on the hit list of extremists because he was investigating some shooting cases.

As soon as the Akali MP, the DC and the police officers reached the spot, another shot was fired in the air. In panic, according to the eyewitnesses, people including some policemen, could

A. S. Atwal

Centre planning to

Headline of Indian Express

Surinder

Jagjit had a sister who passed away when she was only about a year old. After her passing, Surinder was born on 8th September 1940 and was the apple of the eye of her family. She was blessed with particularly good looks and fond of her elder brother, who doted on her. She did her early education wherever her father was posted. After Matriculation, the responsibility of her further education came upon Jagjit and Tejwant, and they got her admitted to Kanya Mahavidyalaya, Jalandhar, for her Intermediate program prior to graduation. Later, she switched to the Gyani program and completed her formal education.

Surinder got married in 1963 to Jagjit Bhullar at Village Bir Puad. Jagjit Bhullar was an inspector in the Punjab Armed Police and was posted in Jalandhar. Jagjit Bhullar was an extremely fine gentleman and was very hardworking. He belonged to Sangrur and had an elder sister who lived in Amritsar with her family. Surinder and Jagjit had three children – Sukhjit (Ashu), Gurpreet (Minna), and Priya (Pria). Jagjit decided to appear for the Punjab Civil Services and worked hard for this. He moved to the Village Bir Puad and toiled ceaselessly until he cleared the exam and got selected. After his training, he was posted in Amritsar for his initial stint in the Civil Services. His next posting was as Sub-Divisional Magistrate, Samrala, where he made quite a name for himself as an efficient officer. It was a sad day when we learned of the passing away of Jagjit Bhullar in Samrala at a young age, leaving behind a very young family.

Surinder moved with her three kids to Nangal, where Jagjit, her brother, was then posted. The family had now become quite large, but everyone adapted well. Soon, Surinder became friendly with Rajbir Dhillon, a family friend. They got married at Jagjit's house in Nangal, and Surinder moved to Chandigarh, taking Priya with her to be with Rajbir. The two boys stayed with Jagjit until Avtar became responsible for bringing up Minna. Minna initially lived with Avtar and Amrita and was subsequently admitted to Punjab Public School, Nabha. Ashu remained a part of Jagjit's family until he finished school and then moved to Phagwara for his graduate studies.

Surinder had two more boys, Navraj (Navi) and Savraj (Savi), with Rajbir. Rajbir continued to stay in Chandigarh until he retired. He then moved to Gurgaon (now called Gurugram) to stay with Navraj and his family. Savraj married Ruth and moved to California, where they now live. Pria moved to the USA at an early age and married Kuljinder (Bunty) Srai early. They have three daughters and live in Seattle, WA. Rajbir passed away on the 10th of September 2021, and Surinder spends her time between the US and India to be with her children and grandchildren.

Ashu had moved to Canada after marriage, which did not last. He continued to stay in Vancouver, British Columbia before finally moving to Mississauga/Brampton in 2004. He initially stayed with Jagjit and Tej until he stabilized in finding a suitable job. Jagjit was an immense help in Ashu's relocation and supported him in every aspect. Meanwhile, Minna had married Mandeep and had two kids, Amol and Udai. Minna unfortunately passed away soon thereafter, and Mandeep got married to Ashu. She moved to Brampton, Ontario, Canada, with her kids, who Ashu adopted.

CHAPTER 6

New Delhi (Kaka Nagar)

In early 1959, Jagjit was allotted house number 28 in Kaka Nagar. This was an independent house and was a welcome move for him since he could now just walk to work and come home for lunch. Their second child, Manoj, was born there on January 11, 1960. Shortly thereafter, they had to move to house number 18 in the same colony as the present one was being converted into an office. Jagjit, meanwhile, got promoted as an Executive Engineer (XEN) and got a bigger house allotted in the same colony. House number 71 was where Juhi was born on October 03, 1962. Due to some administrative reasons, another move was made to house number 96, which was on the upper floor, though this was very temporary as the lower one got vacant and the family moved again.

Since New Delhi was India's capital city, many families from Punjab visited for various reasons. Many of them were from rural areas and were frequently confused and amazed at the facilities they encountered. One individual visiting and staying with Jagjit and Tej saw the refrigerator for the first time in his life and queried Jagjit about the "*Chiitti Almari*" (White Cupboard) he saw in the kitchen. He was really shocked to see that it cooled the items inside and wondered if one could sleep inside during the summer!

Tejwant's father, Atma Singh, lived at the Multi-Story Flats at Safdarjung Road in New Delhi. These were just across the road from the Children's Park at India Gate, a popular place for the kids to visit when they visited their grandparents. Furthermore, there was a television at Atma Singh's place that was a major attraction. Being the only television in the building, it was customary for the other residents to drop in to see the *Chitrahaar* (musical program) on Wednesday evenings and also the movie on Saturdays. So many adults and kids milling around the house could make for a crowd, but the warmth of the family ensured that everyone cooperated and enjoyed the entertainment at the same time.

Jagjit traded his *Rajdoot* motorcycle for a 1962 model Fiat 1100, which had a very distinctive number DLI 210. The family now had much mobility and could visit the city's many other attractions. In March 1969, the family planned a visit to Agra and set course in their car. En route, the car had a single-vehicle collision near Palwal and suffered major damage. But for a broken arm for Manoj and superficial facial injuries for Tejwant, the rest of the family escaped unhurt. After some major repairs, the car was back in service.

Devi Ram was a family friend while they were in Kaka Nagar. He was employed as a Tracer in the Bhakra Designs Directorate, but his talents were elsewhere. He was a wonderful artist who sketched, painted or drew on any medium. He was from Himachal Pradesh and enrolled in the Delhi Polytechnic in the 5-year Fine Arts program while employed. Jagjit used to help him procure art supplies, and Devi Lal responded by churning out many particularly good artworks. Jagjit and Tejwant had a great collection of his early works, some of which remained while they were in India. Many hand-made greeting cards by Devi Lal are still available to the family. Devi Ram was close to the children and was a frequent visitor. He moved back to Himachal Pradesh in 1969, and the family lost touch. However, he did contact Jagjit in 1983 when Avtar was assassinated, but there has not been any contact since then.

Devi Ram Oil Painting 1959

Devi Ram Greeting Card 1962

Kaka Nagar was a very central location in the upcoming metropolis of New Delhi. A residential area for Government officials, it had many facilities like playgrounds, etc. The Delhi Golf Club was just across Mathura Road, and the Delhi Public School was a short walk away. Jagjit and Tejwant's three kids all used to go to this school and typically walked their way there. The Delhi Zoo and the Purana Quila (Old Fort) were also nearby and were frequently visited. The Sundar Nagar Market was the closest shopping complex, and the kids used to look forward to their weekly "Softy" ice cream cone there. The National Stadium was also within walking distance, but the attraction was the Stadium Cinema, where many movies were screened. Another popular place to visit was the Children's Film Society at Sapru House on Barakhamba Road. They screened some nice movies for kids, and we looked forward to being taken there by Jagjit initially and thereafter by Harpal (Pal), who was Tejwant's cousin living with Papaji. Pal was studying and working simultaneously and was close to the kids and indulged them by escorting them to the Children's Park and the movies.

During the 1965 war with Pakistan, there was a general sense of concern, and the rules for the blackout were strictly followed. All windows were covered with dark paper, and minimum illumination was observed during the evenings and nights. Of course, once the sirens went on, all lights were extinguished, and we made our way to the trenches dug up in the parks in front of the houses. During the day, we kids used to play the fool by hiding in the trenches or take turns jumping across them. Manoj was quite little and once fell into a trench while trying to jump across. He suffered a broken arm as a result and spent the next few weeks with it in plaster. Unfortunately, he had another mishap during the accident with the Fiat car in 1968, which broke another arm. Fortunately, he recovered well, and it did not present him with any difficulty in his later years when he took to seam bowling while playing cricket in his youth.

Jagjit had chronic back pain in the early sixties, which was very debilitating. He found it a big challenge while sitting for extended periods of time and while sleeping. He moved to a hard bed, which was a bit different since almost everyone used a niwar cot in those days. Niwar is a thick, narrow, coarse tape made of cotton that is used to bind cots and form a platform for sleeping. These days, one can get niwar in plastic too, but the premise remains the same. He even used to go to Willingdon Hospital (now known as Lok Nayak Jai Prakash Narayan Hospital) for diathermy treatment, but it was not beneficial.

In 1964, he came across Swami Dhirendra Brahmachari, a Yoga teacher who had his ashram in Katra, Jammu, and Kashmir. The swami was a personal teacher of Indira Gandhi, the daughter of Jawaharlal Nehru, the late Prime Minister of India. Indira Gandhi went on to become the Prime Minister herself after the sad demise of Lal Bahadur Shastri, the Prime Minister at Tashkent, after the 1965 war with Pakistan. Jagjit and Tejwant became regular attendees of the classes conducted by Swami Dhirendra Bhramachari at the India Gate lawns. These classes really helped Jagjit, and he could get over the back pain in about 6 months. Jagjit and Tejwant continued to attend these classes as they benefited from them. Even so, after moving to Nangal, Tejwant went for a training course at Katra and got her first certification as a Yoga teacher from there. Her sister Ravinder went along and did the course. After completing the course, Jagjit took us kids along to bring Tejwant back to Nangal.

Jagjit always enjoyed having a cup of tea when the opportunity presented itself. He preferred to have it without sugar as he felt that the brew's taste was compromised by adding it. It was quite a ritual to see him and Tej enjoying their tea together after brewing it in a traditional teapot along with a "tea cozy" and just a dash of milk. This method could prove to be a challenge when he was traveling and on the road. He frequently traveled between New Delhi and Nangal for official work and used the Government car for this. He used to stop at the Haryana Tourism Resort on the outskirts of Karnal to take a tea break and also break the journey. Once when he asked to be served tea without sugar, the cook asked him if it would be okay if he added a bit of sugar to the tea. Jagjit responded humorously that there was so much sugar already at the bottom of the pan being used for preparing the tea that there would be no need to add any more!

Jagjit was an active member of the Lions Club in New Delhi. He regularly attended their meetings and contributed his time and expertise to many of the charitable activities that the organization conducted. Also, he was a member of the Jat Sikh Association (JSA), a body that was highly active in the integration of the Sikh community into the mainstream in Delhi. This was important since there were a lot of problems after the partition and the resettlement of the refugees who came from Pakistan. The JSA organized an annual day during the summer to synchronize with the summer vacations for the school children. Normally, these events were held in public parks and were self-catered, but the organizers provided the mangoes. These picnics were looked forward to, and they used to culminate in a mango-eating orgy as there were no limits on what one could eat.

A fallout of Jagjit's association with JSA was that he became a member of a cooperative house-building society, which was allotted land to build a colony for its members on the eastern bank of the Yamuna River. In the sixties, there were all open fields, and the only built-up area was at Shahdara situated just across the Yamuna bridge near the Red Fort. I remember a trip we took to see the planned colony. There were only open fields, and there was a big open drain that carried the sewage into the River Yamuna. Of course, there has been huge development with roads and flyovers built since then, but the stinky open drain has not gone away anywhere, and it is a breeding ground for mosquitoes which really make their presence felt! The Yamuna Barrage near ITO was to be the take-off point eastwards to open new colonies, and the city expanded. This decision of Jagjit's was very strategic as many years down the line when it came to constructing his retirement house, the plot of land purchased at that time was crucial for its implementation.

CHAPTER 7

ONSITE HYDEL PROJECTS

Water, the lifeblood of civilizations, has always been a crucial factor in India's development. Though Bhakra was the first major hydel project of independent India, the Beas-Sutlej Link Project was a corollary to this mission of managing its water resources for economic growth and agricultural prosperity. Connecting two mighty rivers, the Beas and the Sutlej, this ambitious project embodied a harmonious blend of engineering, vision, and necessity.

Bhakra

The Bhakra Dam project is one of India's most significant and ambitious hydroelectric and irrigation infrastructure projects. Located on the Sutlej River in the northern state of Himachal Pradesh (though Nangal is in Punjab), this dam is among the highest gravity dams in the world, standing at approximately 226 meters (741 feet). It was constructed with the primary goals of providing irrigation water, generating hydroelectric power, and managing flood control in the Sutlej Basin. The idea for the Bhakra Dam was first proposed in the 1900s, with initial planning beginning in the 1940s. However, construction only commenced after India's independence in 1948 and was completed in 1963. The project was inaugurated by then Prime Minister Jawaharlal Nehru, who called it one of the "temples of modern India" because of its contribution to the country's agricultural and industrial growth. Though Bhakra Dam did the job of optimizing the flow of the Sutlej for irrigation and power generation, the ever-growing demand for these resources forced the planners to look for ingenious ways to ensure that the Gobind Sagar reservoir did not reach critical levels, especially during the summer when the demand was the highest. The planners came up with the idea of using the excess flow of the Beas River and diverting it to the Sutlej for augmentation.

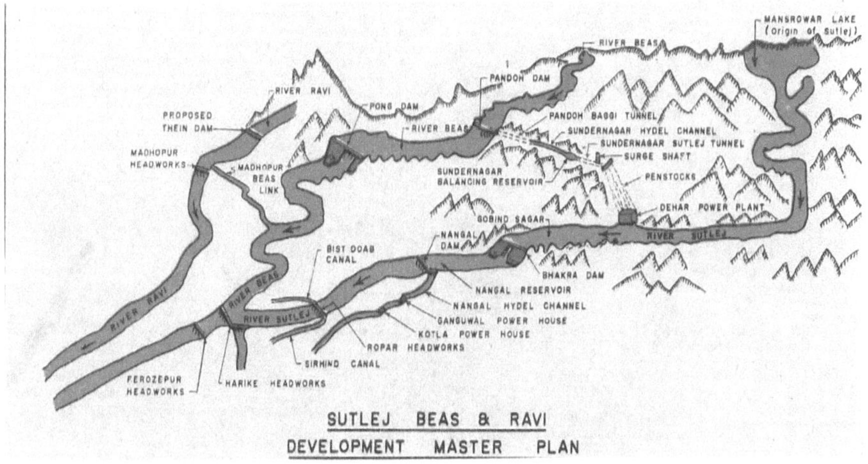

Bhakra Complex

Beas-Sutlej Link Project

The origins of the Beas-Sutlej Link (BSL) Project can be traced back to the Indus Waters Treaty of 1960, which allocated the waters of the Ravi, Beas, and Sutlej rivers to India. Recognizing the potential of the Beas River, a plan was devised to divert its surplus waters into the Sutlej River basin to optimize water usage and augment irrigation in northern India. Work on the project commenced in the 1960s and culminated in its completion in 1977.

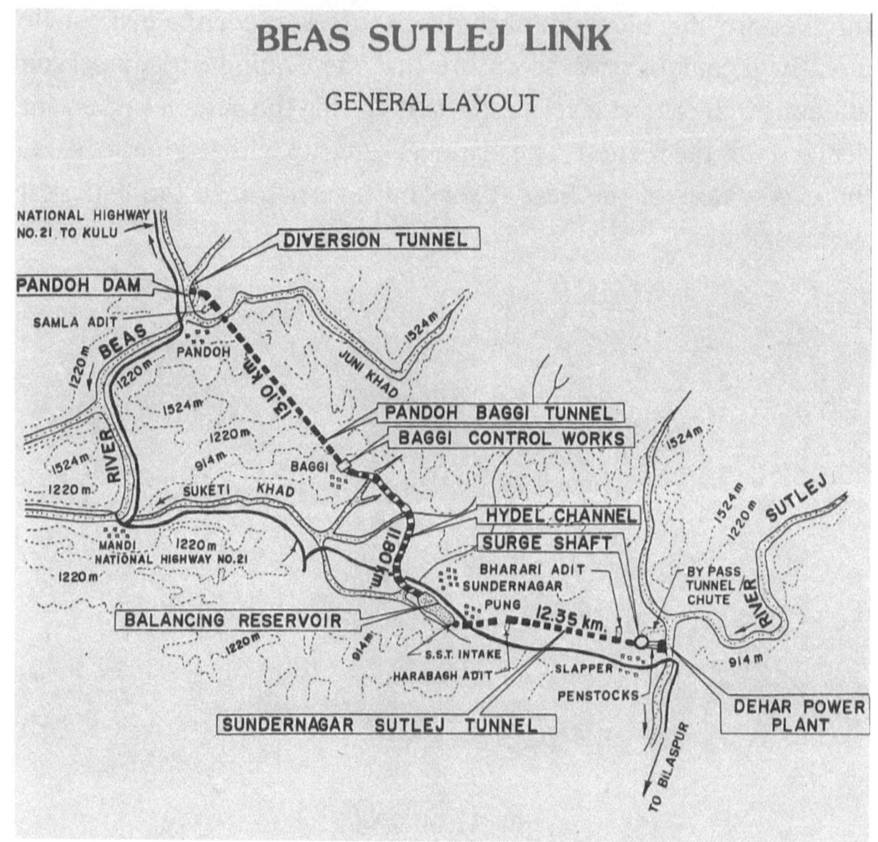

Beas Sutlej Link

The Beas-Sutlej Link (BSL) Project is a major inter-basin water transfer project designed to divert water from the Beas River to the Sutlej River. At the heart of the Beas-Sutlej Link Project lies the Pandoh Dam, a diversion dam constructed on the Beas River in Himachal Pradesh. Located primarily in Himachal Pradesh, the project aims to maximize the utility of water resources in the region by transferring water from the relatively abundant Beas Basin to the Sutlej Basin, where it can be more effectively used for irrigation, power generation, and regional development. The Beas-Sutlej Link diverts water from the Beas River into the Sutlej River through a series of tunnels and canals. One of the primary engineering feats of the project is the 13.1-kilometer-long Pandoh-Baggi tunnel, which connects the Beas River to the Pandoh Dam.

The water is then conveyed through a series of tunnels and open channels to the Dehar Powerhouse, where it is used to generate electricity before being discharged into the Sutlej River. The Dehar Powerhouse has an installed capacity of around 990 megawatts, contributing a significant amount of hydroelectric power to the national grid. The Beas-Sutlej Link has significantly enhanced irrigation across Punjab, Haryana, and Rajasthan. Augmenting the Sutlej's flow ensures a stable water supply for agriculture, enabling farmers to cultivate multiple crops annually. The project has transformed arid and semi-arid regions into fertile agricultural lands, supporting India's Green Revolution and ensuring food security.

The entire project entailed some unique engineering initiatives, the main one being the strata of the mountains being very unstable and using complex techniques for the construction. The Pandoh-Baggi tunnel was a major piece of the whole complex, and drilling into the mountain began at both ends. The water pressure was enormous, so the tunnel had to be designed for this and the subsequent erosion during continuous use. The precise drilling and blasting ensured that when the tunnels were completed and met in the middle, they were merely inches apart. Another unique feature was the establishment of a surge shaft that was incorporated into the tunnels as they brought the water down to the Dehar Powerhouse. This vertical shaft was 125 meters high and was located at the end of the tunnel. It was designed to handle any backflow due to the sudden shutdown of the power plant and avoid tunnel rupture due to the water hammer effect. We were privy to an event when this was activated, and the whole valley was really showered with a fine spray like a fountain!

Surge Shaft Operation

CHAPTER 8

MOVE TO NANGAL

1969 saw Jagjit posted to Nangal, which was the original place where the offices and the residences of the personnel working at the Bhakra Dam complex were located. Though the Bhakra Dam had been completed, some projects were still to be integrated. The move to Nangal was full of challenges for the family. Having been used to life in the big city of New Delhi, Nangal was a one-horse town. The colony only catered for the residents who worked on the hydel projects. There was a small market and only one movie theater, which had seen better days. There was an Officer's Club, which was the center of social activity. It screened movies on the weekends on the lawns and provided much-needed entertainment. There was a pool where all of us learned to swim. The only school that provided some quality education was located across the River Sutlej in the township of Naya Nangal, and the site of the Fertilizer Factory. We kids were admitted to that school, and the boys used bicycles to travel there. This was a fair distance, and the winter season did pose some challenges, but it was compensated during the crossing of the River Sutlej at Nangal Dam. We used to stop midway and admire the construction and the Bhakra canal take-off at that location.

We had initially moved to a small temporary accommodation at River View Road once we arrived in Nangal Township since accommodation fitting Jagjit's status was unavailable. This was an ad-hoc arrangement for a few months and once a suitable house was made available, we moved to 4, Town Hall Road, close to the River Sutlej and the Officers Club. This was a large house with a garage at the rear and came along with a servant's quarter, complete with toilets and a kitchen. Throughout the five years we stayed there, there was never an occasion that we had a servant staying in our house. There was a large, fenced compound with many fruit trees like mango, jamun, mulberry etc. There were a couple of fields around the house, and this gave many ideas to Jagjit and Tejwant. They planted many crops there, since there was an abundant water supply for irrigating them. Wheat, sugarcane, vegetables, maize, etc., and a lot of green fodder were harvested.

The acquisition of a buffalo was the next project. As an eleven-year-old lad, I was sent to Samrala, where Jagjit's brother-in-law was now the Sub-Divisional Magistrate. I still remember my dad giving me a thousand odd rupees (this was a huge amount in those times) and putting me on a bus. I was taken along to the cattle fair by my uncle, the late Jagjit Bhullar, and I sort of selected a brown buffalo and escorted it back to Nangal on a truck. It was the first attempt of a home dairy, and my mother Tej soon took charge. She learned how to milk it, and we children really enjoyed the end products. There was yet another buffalo that got added, and the brownie and blackie served us well for a long time. Later, broiler and layer chicks were brought, and a chicken coop was constructed to cater to the poultry. There were some mishaps too, like once when a mongoose got into the chicken coop and slaughtered many birds. Another time, one of the buffaloes (blackie) broke her leg and slowly withered away and had to be put to sleep. Though we had Damodar Ram (Jagjit's peon from the office on a part-time job) to help with the top work for the buffaloes, we all contributed as a family to feeding and looking after the livestock.

Jagjit had many colleagues at Nangal who had studied with him in the Civil Engineering program at Roorkee. Friendships were revived, and it became a busy social life. We were close to a couple of families, and dinner invitations were aplenty. The family of Ram Nath Hoon, wife Reva, and daughter Shivani (she is Juhi's age) lived two houses away, and we were frequent visitors. Reva's brother, Bhappie Sonie, was a film producer/director, and he brought along his stars and film production company for some movies like Jheel Ke Us Paar starring Dharmendra and Mumtaz, and Chalta Purza starring Rajesh Khanna and Praveen Babi at another time. We got to interact with the stars and see the film shooting up close on the sets. Jagat and Saroj Mehra were another couple who were part of the group that used to socialize a lot. Jagjit was also highly active socially and attended many bridge sessions at the Officers Club. He had an exceptionally good memory that helped him plan and enjoy the game. Sometimes, we had events at the Officers Club like Whist Drive, and Jagjit used to invariably be part of the winning team. Jagjit had always been a sports person, and though the opportunity for playing hockey was not available, he used to participate in a friendly game of cricket among the officers, where he used to keep wickets.

Mehras, Hoons and Atwals

After the passing away of Jagjit Bhullar and the remarriage of Jagjit's sister Surinder, their elder son Ashu joined Jagjit's family. This responsibility was happily taken on by Jagjit and Tejwant, and Ashu became an integral part of their family. This continued until Ashu completed school in Chandigarh, and then Jagjit's father decided that he would take over the responsibility of his further graduate studies. To meet the cost of education, some parts of the ancestral land at Village Bir Puad were sold off.

Nangal was the place where Jagjit's kids, especially I, really grew. Being a teenager, at a very impressionable age, I needed a role model to look up to. What better than one's own father who was around all the time to talk with, discuss things, and most of all, provide guidance. At that age, one is torn on the choice of one's career and growing up among my father's peers who were exclusively all engineers, there was an expectation that the kids would follow suit. The Fertilizer Corporation of India (FCI) Model Higher School at Naya Nangal was the only school that fitted the bill for quality education as it had an education curriculum that was exclusively in English.

There was the requirement to study a second language of Hindi, for which one had to clear an exam in Grade 10. In addition, there was another language of Punjabi to be studied, the exam of which needed to be passed by the end of Grade 8. This was one language I had never encountered, and it became a challenge to learn the script and grammar. In the end, through sheer persistence, I passed the Punjabi exam with good grades, and I am glad that I can still read and write the language. The school also provided many opportunities to go on excursions to hill stations and other places of historical importance. An annual Shankar's Art Competition was organized at the Modern School grounds in New Delhi, and our school used to send talented students to participate in it. I was fortunate to be selected several times for this, and I still hold cherished memories of those trrips. All this was possible due to the encouragement and funding provided by my parents since we had to pay for our travel, board, and lodging.

Along the southern bank of the River Sutlej and close to our house on Townhall Road were two places of religious importance. The Sikh temple of Gurudwara Ghat Sahib shared the boundary wall with the Laxmi Narayan Mandir for the Hindu faith. Many religious functions used to be organized there, and they overlapped frequently. Each institution used to raise the level of the loudspeakers to outdo the other. I used to get up early in the morning to study before going to school, and I did not need any alarm clock for this since the priests ensured that everyone living in the vicinity woke up when they blew into the microphone to test it before commencing the morning prayers.

National Defence Academy

I needed to decide in my final year in school when I was in Grade 11 for the final Higher Secondary examination about the career I wished to pursue, and I did have a conversation with my father about this. He did give me a lot of options after doing his research. Not much information was available, barring word of mouth or the newspapers and magazines. He nevertheless got me the information that would get me going toward applying for the entrance examinations. It was quite a process with timelines for submitting applications, filling them out, fixing photographs for the admit cards, and deciding the examination centers since none were close to where we stayed. All these had to be filled out very accurately, and the trips had to be planned. Since I had sort of decided to apply for the National Defence Academy (NDA), the only center close by was in New Delhi, and the date was in December 1973. My gravitating toward the NDA and life in uniform could be partially attributed to my conversations with Jagjit's brother Avtar, who had spent the early part of his career in the

Army as an Emergency Commission officer. My choice of Air Force was based solely on the advertisement for NDA, which indicated that the Air Force paid the highest since it included the flying pay!

The IIT (Indian Institute of Technology) exam was in Chandigarh around the same time, and the one for Merchant Navy (TS Rajendra) was also in Chandigarh. My father planned to accompany me for these trips to ensure that we had a place to stay, and he took take care of the administrative arrangements so that I remained focused on the actual exams. He was very diligent in the planning and ensured that he took care of the minutest detail. I did clear the NDA Entrance Exam and proceeded to Fazilka, where Avtar was commanding a BSF Battalion to prepare for the Air Force Selection Board interview. The Higher Secondary result came out in April 1974, and I did well, and so did so many of my batch mates from school.

I joined the 52nd Course of the NDA as an Air Force cadet and was in the Science Stream, with French as the Foreign Language. The training was tough initially since I had no exposure to boarding school. Leaving the security of one's home at the age of 16+ and exposed to a new way of living was a matter of survival. I had to reach out many a time to my father via letters to get a word of encouragement and support. He always had my back and responded with frequent letters. Once, I was very discouraged to have not made it through a particular exercise that involved jumping from the 7-meter board into the pool since I was afraid of the height, and he responded with that famous verse from the "Guns of Navarone", and I quote verbatim *"Andrea was afraid. Andrea is afraid. Andrea is always afraid. That is why I have lived so long. And why so many have died. They were not so afraid as I. They were not afraid of everything a man could be afraid of, there was always something they forgot to fear, to guard against. But Andrea was afraid of everything, and he forgot nothing. It is as simple as that. There are no brave men and cowardly men in the world, my son. There are only brave men. To be born, live, and die takes courage enough in itself and more than enough. We are all brave men and afraid, and what the world calls a brave man, he, too, is brave and afraid like all the rest of us. Only he is brave for five minutes longer. Or sometimes ten minutes, or twenty minutes, or the time it takes a man sick and bleeding and afraid to climb a cliff."*

7th June 1977 was the day I was waiting since that was the day of the Passing Out Parade (POP) of our course from the NDA. It is a tradition that the parents of the cadets of the passing out course are invited to attend the ceremony. For this, invitations are sent out, and interested parents indicate if they will be attending. I was extremely fortunate that Jagjit and Tej decided to make the trip from Chandigarh. They even brought Manoj, Juhi, and Shivani along for this. Their stay arrangements were made in the Academy itself, and they attended many functions. It was great to have my entire family there for the occasion. After the ceremonies, we went to Mumbai (then Bombay) and stayed a couple of days there. Madhavi (Shivani's aunt) organized the stay arrangements, and we went sightseeing to many of the local attractions in Mumbai.

Family Get together at Moga 1977

CHAPTER 9

MOVE TO CHANDIGARH

Jagjit was promoted as a Superintending engineer, and not having a suitable position in Nangal, he was posted to the Design Office in Chandigarh. In the summer of 1974, the family moved to Chandigarh, and I was the happiest person to accompany the luggage truck, which had our belongings. Since no Government accommodation was available, Jagjit rented the upper floor of a house in Sector 35B. I left shortly thereafter to join the NDA. Jagjit had his office in Sector 18, and there was a fair bit of travel for Manoj, Juhi, and Ashu to go to school. Therefore, Jagjit located and rented an independent house in Sector 18A. This location was convenient for everyone and was the residence for the next two years until an appropriate Government accommodation was allotted at house No. 9, Sector 7-A. This house became the focal point for the family as it was large enough to cater to visitors, and it was a large lot with some fruit trees. The location was perfect as it was just steps away from the Sukhna Lake, which was an attraction for everyone. The schools and, subsequently, the colleges were very easily accessible for the kids.

Jagjit had nicely settled down in his new assignment and continued working with the Hydel Office of the Punjab Government. In 1966, the state of Punjab had been reorganized as Punjab and Haryana. The sharing of the waters of the Sutlej downstream of the Bhakra Dam between these states was a major issue. Consequently, the Sutlej Yamuna Link (SYL) canal concept was developed. Some portion had been allotted to the state of Delhi and some to the state of Rajasthan via the Indira Gandhi Canal. Due to the ever-growing demand for water for the increasing population and agriculture, major discussions were concurrently carried on at various levels. Jagjit was mandated to represent the state of Punjab at these forums. Still, since this was a political rather than an engineering solution, the debate dragged on, and, unfortunately, this has still not been resolved. The need for reliance on canal-driven irrigation is even more as the groundwater continues to be exploited, and the water table continues to plummet. Haryana completed its share of the SYL canal, but Punjab never completed almost 100 km of it to allow the waters of the Sutlej to flow.

Shortly thereafter, Jagjit was assigned to the Ranjit Sagar Dam project while still in Chandigarh. The Ranjit Sagar Dam, also known as Thein Dam, was conceptualized to dam the waters of the River Ravi in northern Punjab and divert them southwards to add to Punjab's irrigation potential. Since the waters of the River Ravi had continued to flow into Pakistan downstream of the Mukerian headworks, storage of the waters at the Ranjit Sagar Dam would enable regulated flow and release of the snow-fed river in the summer months when the demand for irrigation was the highest. Jagjit had to travel frequently to the dam location and had a car allocated to him from the Government pool. He had a very capable driver, Mohan Singh (affectionately called Mohan Singh Bhaisaab), who had spent some time in the Indian Army.

Meanwhile, after completing my training at NDA at Khadakwasla in June 1977 I completed the initial flying training at the Elementary Flying School at Bidar in December 1977. Followed by advanced training at the Air Force Academy at Dundigal, Hyderabad, I was commissioned as an officer in the Indian Air Force in July 1978. After more training stints at Kalaikunda, West Bengal, and Tezpur in Assam, I was posted to a frontline fighter squadron in Halwara, Punjab. I was in Pune in late 1980 for more training and met Linda, and sparks flew. It was a foregone conclusion that we were to be married, and when I broached the subject with Jagjit and Tejwant, I was unsure of their reaction, but it was Jagjit who unhesitatingly gave his blessing for this. Our marriage was solemnized on May 28, 1982, via a civil ceremony at Jagjit's house by the magistrate who came over for the occasion. There was a reception at the same location where family, friends, and many officers and their wives from my squadron came by bus to join the festivities. Manoj had already left for Canada for his postgraduate program, and it had only been made possible through a generous contribution by Jagjit and Tejwant. We were extremely fortunate that Linda's dad, Emanuel, and her sister, Regina, could join us for this occasion.

Silver Wedding Anniversary

A couple of months later, I was posted to Ambala with a change of aircraft and was initially allotted temporary accommodation. Ambala, being rather close to Chandigarh, Jagjit could manage to visit us at regular intervals, and we could make the trip to meet them. It was on April 25, 1983, that Linda and I were in Chandigarh when the terrible news of Avtar's assassination was conveyed to Jagjit. He was very shaken, and after some transport arrangements were made, we all traveled to Jalandhar with Amrita. It was a sad occasion, and Jagjit was hit extremely hard, but being the strong person he was, he took charge of the situation and organized everything. Jagjit's parents, Hari Singh and Beant Kaur were heartbroken, and Amrita and Harbir needed the most support. The family rallied, and as messages of condolences poured in from the then Prime Minister Indira Gandhi downwards, Avtar was laid to rest. After this, the family moved to Chandigarh to grieve and organize for the future. A big prayer meeting was held at Jagjit's house in Chandigarh and many dignitaries from the Governor downwards attended. All official support was promised for Amrita and Harbir, but as is normally the case, promises are not forthcoming easily. It was only through Jagjit's persistent efforts to follow up, that the decision was made to grant Amrita a full pension and a job in the Punjab Civil Services (PCS). Harbir's admission to a prominent school in Chandigarh was a result of Jagjit's efforts. Amrita and Harbir started living with Jagjit and Tejwant in their house in Chandigarh while Amrita trained for the PCS. Even though her initial job profile did not entitle her as such, Jagjit persevered for the allotment of the same house where he had been staying (house No. 9, Sector 7-A) to Amrita, knowing that his retirement from Government service upon reaching the age of fifty-eight would be coming up in a couple of years.

In addition, he was offered a consultancy position for an Indian government-aided hydel project in Afghanistan. Since the major administrative arrangements for settling Amrita and Harbir were made, Jagjit and Tejwant decided that it was time to make a move, as there was a substantial financial uptick due to this international assignment. They moved to Delhi and took up residence in the upstairs apartment of Avtar Berar (Tejwant's cousin), who had meanwhile retired from the Indian Army and constructed his house at 194 Hargobind Enclave, a colony in East Delhi. Incidentally, since Jagjit had also become a member of the colony while in the Jat Sikh Association (JSA), he had been allotted a plot of land at 68 Hargobind Enclave, which was just down the lane from Avtar Berar's residence. Jagjit traveled to Kabul on the assignment, and Tejwant and Juhi started living in Hargobind Enclave.

CHAPTER 10

AFGHANISTAN

Afghanistan was under the Soviet occupation at that time. The project that Jagjit was contracted to work for was the Salma Hydel Dam project. This entire project was contracted to Water and Power Consultancy Services (India) Ltd (WAPCOS). It was located at an aerial distance of almost 500 km west of Kabul, the capital of Afghanistan. Land travel was out of the question as there was a large presence of the Taliban in the countryside. Though technically the project planning work was being carried on, extremely limited work on the ground could be conducted during the Soviet occupation. Therefore, Jagjit found himself mainly confined to Kabul, though he did travel occasionally to the site itself. This travel was by Soviet military helicopters, and there was always the risk of being attacked enroute by the Taliban fighters armed with shoulder-fired Stinger Surface-to-Air Missiles (SAMs).

The Salma Dam, located in the Herat Province of western Afghanistan, is crucial in providing irrigation and electricity to the region. Given Afghanistan's largely agricultural economy, this dam is vital for water storage and agricultural productivity, particularly in the arid and semi-arid regions of the country. It allows for year-round irrigation, improving crop yields and supporting food security for local communities. The construction of the Salma Dam was a massive challenge. The project faced delays, and many logistical difficulties arose from transporting materials and labor through difficult terrain. Furthermore, maintaining such large infrastructure in a conflict zone requires careful planning and resilience.

Jagjit became friends with the Chief Engineer from the Afghan side, and they spent many evenings together. Jagjit was educated in Urdu during his school days and could also communicate easily in Persian. In fact, he and his father, Hari Singh, used to write letters to each other in Urdu. Consequently, Jagjit enjoyed Urdu poetry and knew the finer nuances conveyed by the poet. Being largely confined to the hotel and not able to find Indian food, he took to experimenting with cooking. Communication with Tejwant back in Delhi was sporadic, and he was missing home and his family. The diet and the uncertainty in that environment started taking a toll on his health. He was losing weight, which was subsequently diagnosed as due to having Graves' disease or hyperthyroidism. In addition, he was also pre-diabetic. This condition was not genetic since he was the first member of his family to have been diagnosed as such.

Tejwant and Juhi decided to visit Kabul in May/June 1984 to spend time with Jagjit. The city was largely safe, but there was a large presence of Soviet troops. Most of their time was spent in the hotel premises with Jagjit. They stayed there for a couple of weeks, and soon after their return, Operation Blue Star was conducted at the Golden Temple in Amritsar between June 1st to 10th to rid the religious shrine of the terrorists who wanted a separate state of Khalistan to be created for the Sikhs of Punjab. This Army operation, ordered by Prime Minister Indira Gandhi, did not go well with the supporters of the movement, and her Sikh bodyguards assassinated her at her residence in New Delhi on October 31, 1984. This unleashed an anti-Sikh wave that spread quickly to many parts of the country. Angry mobs descended upon individuals, businesses, and places of worship of the Sikhs. Countless innocent people lost their lives, and it was understood that there was implicit support of the law authorities for this pogrom. Tejwant was in the Hargobind Enclave at that time, and there was a large mob that came with malafide intent. Fortunately, some ex-military officers resided in the colony and had their personal firearms. The mob did manage to attack the gurudwara only and set some parts of it on fire, but the residents of the colony defended well with threats of firing in the air and thus escaped with no loss to persons or property.

That year, in April, I had a flying accident, and I had to eject from a Jaguar aircraft. I escaped with no injuries, but the aircraft was destroyed. After the inquiry and waiting for the decision, I was sent to Leh since a Operation Meghdoot had started on the Siachen Glacier bordering Pakistan. Linda joined me after a couple of weeks, and since it was the summer season, we managed to see a fair bit of the local and nearby attractions. In July, I got orders to move to Secunderabad to convert to helicopters. Linda and I moved for a six-month course and after completion, I was posted at Hasimara in West Bengal.

CHAPTER 11

RETURN TO INDIA

Since there was not much going on regarding the progress on the Salma Dam in Afghanistan, Jagjit returned to India in early 1985 and assumed his position with the Punjab Government at Chandigarh. He was now deputed to the Shahpur Kandi hydel project, which was essentially the irrigation take-off downstream of the Ranjit Sagar Dam. He continued staying at the Sector 7 house, which was now allotted to Amrita, whereas Tejwant and Juhi were in Delhi. Juhi had completed her MSc and Bachelor of Education program in Chandigarh and started a job in Delhi.

Juhi's wedding was solemnized in June 1985 with Gurpreet (Tony) Chahal at the Sector 7 house in Chandigarh. The Chahal family lived in Canada, and Juhi started the paperwork to join her husband there as soon as possible as she was soon expecting a baby. She reached Canada in January 1986, and her daughter Tania was born on March 23, 1986.

Jagjit was promoted to Chief Engineer and took on the responsibility of the Designs Directorate of the Thein Dam (also known as Ranjit Sagar Dam). Tejwant and Jagjit decided that although Jagjit was to be physically located in Chandigarh for his job, and his retirement was forthcoming in about two years' time when he turned 58, it was high time to get the house constructed on the plot they had in Hargobind Enclave in Delhi. Therefore, Tejwant continued to rent the upper floor of her brother Avtar Berar's house and supervised the construction. The plans were drawn by Namita, a very competent architect in Chandigarh. She was the daughter of Mr. Agnihotri, who was Jagjit's senior in the Punjab Government Hydel Department.

68 Hargobind Enclave was almost adjacent to the Vikas Marg and backed onto the road where important facilities like the main Post Office, Railway Reservation Center, and many Hospitals were located. Though the plot was comparatively small at about 200 sq m, the design of the split-level house gave it the appearance of a larger one. Large windows for sunlight and ducted walls for central air conditioning were incorporated for the efficient flow of air. The construction of the house took the most of 1986 and was ready to be moved in during the early part of 1987. A path (Reading of the Guru Granth Sahib) followed by a small party for "Grah Pravesh" was organized, and Manoj also came down from Canada for this event.

Jagjit retired from the Punjab Government on superannuation as Chief Engineer in December 1987. He received a very warm send-off from his department and colleagues, and he moved to Delhi, looking forward to a life of retirement. It soon became apparent to Jagjit that he could not sit idle doing anything as a retired person. Therefore, he took employment with REDECON, a company that offered contractual works for many major projects. Jagjit was involved in the designing of the Narmada Canal, a major irrigation project in Madhya Pradesh and Gujarat. Though he was based in Delhi, he had to frequently make trips to Vadodara for onsite consultations and coordination.

Meanwhile, Juhi was having some issues with her spouse and his family in Canada. Her brother Manoj had become friendly with Harbir, the sister of Gurpreet (Juhi's spouse). Jagjit and Tej had brought up their kids to be very independent in their outlook, and the subservient behavior expected by her in-laws found Juhi wanting, and she found it extremely difficult to adjust to this situation. The indifferent attitude of her brother, who had prioritized his relationship with Harbir, also did not help. It was a very cold and dark wintery morning when Juhi was made to leave her house with her infant daughter, Tania. Fortunately, her uncles Kuku and Billoo (Tejwant's brothers) lived in the city and took her home for shelter and subsequent follow-up.

Jagjit and Tej were very much affected by this turn of events. As alluded earlier, Jagjit had been diagnosed with hyperthyroidism and was under treatment at INMAS (Institute of Nuclear Medicine and Allied Sciences), Timarpur in Delhi. This premier institute, primarily run by the Defence Services, also caters to the treatment of patients with chronic diseases by way of nuclear medicines. Jagjit was treated there with radioactive iodine, which effectively reduced the size of his overactive thyroid gland and ensured that his disease was controlled with a dosage of synthetic thyroxin. This effectively controlled his weight loss, hypertension, and diabetes to a certain extent. The worry about the situation with Juhi also made matters worse.

Manoj and Harbir got married, and they welcomed their daughter Ambika on January 2nd, 1989. They also resided in Mississauga and remained in touch with Jagjit and Tej. Ambika went to a private school, completed her BBA/MBA, and has had a successful career. She is now married to Bobby and has a son named Rudra.

CHAPTER 12

MOVE TO CANADA

Jagjit and Tej decided to go to Canada to provide emotional support to Juhi and Tania. They did manage to resolve the issues, but it became apparent that a legal separation between Juhi and her spouse was the only way out. Things were set into motion, and after a few months, they returned to India and applied for immigration to Canada to be with Juhi and assist her in settling down with her life. They were issued a permanent resident visa in January 1990, and after settling all the paperwork and closing the house in Delhi, they moved to Canada and landed there on June 17, 1990. Juhi had a small house in Milton and gladly welcomed her parents. They settled in Canada quickly since there was a large family presence and they had spent some time the previous year. While having had a very responsible job and career in India, Jagjit found that he could not apply his experience to use and secure a decent job. Tejwant, in the meanwhile, had picked a job to keep herself busy and to bring in some financial support for the small family.

Jagjit spent much time with his granddaughter Tania, who fondly addressed him as Pa. He used to walk down to drop her off at school and pick her up after school. He used to take her to the park and to the local community center for swimming lessons. He spent time with her playing board games or just reading together. He told her stories about his education, career as a civil engineer, and the journey of planning and constructing the many hydel projects he had been associated with. Tania was very fond of him, and she was motivated toward a career as a civil engineer, for which she studied and eventually became a civil engineer after graduating from the University of Waterloo. Tania also accompanied Jagjit during a visit to India in December 2000 when she was just 14 years old. Jagjit took her to many places to meet relatives and expose her to some notable attractions.

Jagjit tried to get a job in his line and did secure one for a brief period when he got a consulting position with the Pine Portage Generation Station of Ontario Hydro. Not well-suited to doing jobs in retail, he sought some volunteering positions with community organizations. Juhi moved to Mississauga, enabling Jagjit to use public transit and volunteer his time with community organizations.

Tejwant, who had not had a real full-time job while in India, was encouraged by Jagjit to seek one, and she did make a career of it. She got her PSW certification and was fully involved in her work at the Allendale Long-Term Care Facility in Milton. She also had never driven a car. Through his encouragement, she learned it and became independent. I would go on to say that even though she had been very industrious earlier, she became even more so in Canada. It was entirely due to Jagjit's encouragement and support that Tej achieved all this, and it helped her immensely to be independent after Jagjit gave up driving due to his medical condition. Currently, this is really a huge advantage that she still drives and remains independent, while negotiating the roads even in the harshest conditions of the Canadian winter.

Jagjit was close to his father-in-law, Atma Singh, for whom he had utmost regard. Atma Singh resided in Mississauga with his son Billoo and daughter-in-law Pimmi. He was very well-read, passionate about knowledge, and always keen to learn new things. He was addicted to doing the "Jumble Word" in the Toronto Star daily. Unfortunately, his eyesight was failing due to macular degeneration and the detaching of the retina. This was a big setback for him, but he continued to read with the help of a thick magnifying glass. Jagjit made it a point to visit frequently to see Atma Singh and engage him in long conversations about many topics. Atma Singh had an extensive knowledge of plants and their maintenance and gave good advice to Jagjit for caring for the many indoor plants in Jagjit's condo. This proved to be helpful, and they really started thriving and many are still around in the same location. Unfortunately, Atma Singh passed away in 2002, and his widow Amrit Kaur continued to reside with Billoo and Pimmi. Jagjit continued to make frequent visits to meet her and keep her engaged. Jagjit was very caring and respectful, and he was very fond of his mother-in-law, Amrit Kaur. She had a special place for Jagjit and enjoyed his company. They spent long hours reminiscing about old times and the good and the not-so-good events that had taken place in the family.

Some of his best friends were his brothers-in-law. He was especially close to them, and family gatherings were memorable. As kids, we looked forward to visiting them, and he ensured we met them frequently to build relationships. I would affirm that his approach just made for closer relationships, and the bonds that formed then have endured since. Tej's cousin Avtar Singh, who had become part of the family after the sad loss of his parents and siblings during the partition, had served in the Indian Army and had settled down in Hargobind Enclave in Delhi. Jagjit and he had a special relationship, which continued to grow when Jagjit and Tej built their house in the same colony. Avtar's wife Manjit came from a family from Phagwara, and this further increased the closeness. Avtar helped immensely when there was any requirement, like when Juhi required her parents presence in Canada after her marriage did not work out. Avtar was also the driving force behind the pilgrimage by Jagjit to the Sikh holy site of Hemkund Sahib in 1994.

Meanwhile, all Tej's brothers had moved and settled down in Canada through Denmark. Jogi, the eldest, was married to Sukhwinder and was the driving force in the setting up of Vitrex Ceramics.

This was the same name under which he used to operate a similar enterprise in Moga prior to his move abroad. Jogi was on board the Air India Kanishka flight that was blown up enroute from Toronto to New Delhi on 23 June 1985. Sukhwinder managed to raise her three daughters by herself but succumbed to illness in 2024. Kuku was next, and he is married to Harvinder (Guddi) and they reside in Burlington, Ontario. Billoo married his next-door sweetheart Paramjeet (Pimmi), and they live in Mississauga, Ontario. Vitrex Ceramics was a family-run enterprise; the three brothers and their spouses helped in the operations. Due to increased cheap imports from China and diminishing sales margins, the factory was forced to close after being in operation for almost 25 years.

Hrideshwar Singh Berar, Jagjit,
Harinder Singh Berar 2010

Mothers Day 2010

Further, Tej's sisters, Baby and Bhopi, moved to Canada with their families and settled in Burlington. The large family presence just increased interaction between Jagjit and his immediate and extended family. Almost all events, like birthdays and anniversaries, were celebrated, and it was an unwritten rule that one was obligated to attend. Everyone participated with enthusiasm, and a summer family picnic was the highlight. The annual event normally occurred initially at Niagara Falls and later at the Bronte Creek Provincial Park grounds in Burlington and was planned well. Responsibilities were given out and happily accepted. The tradition continues to this day with many family members adding their friends to the attendees list.

Jagjit Singh Atwal, Dr Anoop Singh Sandhu, Dr Balwant Singh Tung,
Baldev Singh Khaihra 1984

Jagjit was a model for many members of the village of Bir Puad, some of whom are now settled in Canada. They looked up to him for support and guidance, since he was one of the few who had worked hard and been educated. He always reached out to them and went out of his way to participate in times of happiness and sorrow. He inspired many to move to this country and make a good life for themselves. They sought his advice and were reassured that they could rely upon him if they needed help. His visits to his ancestral village were looked forward to by the residents, and he tried to settle many disputes that were simmering among families due to trivial issues.

Linda and I welcomed Pia and Samay into our family in 1990 and 1992 respectively, providing us much joy and happiness. Jagjit and Tej really engaged with them and relished their role as grandparents while staying with us during their visits to India. Even though Jagjit and Tej lived half a world away, their presence was sufficient to influence Pia and Samay. Subsequently, when we immigrated to

Canada in October 2004, Jagjit and Tej made place for us in their relatively small condo. This helped us immensely in settling down quickly in a new country. Pia and Samay had a lot of respect for their "Dadaji" and engaged with him during our frequent meetups. Pia is now married to Clarence, while Samay is married to Amaryllis, and they are raising their families.

CHAPTER 13

JAGJIT'S PERSONALITY

Jagjit had a strong belief in holding on to values and ethics. He was very honest and had absolute integrity. Even though he held positions of importance where he could exert influence on the procurement of materials and contracts for financial considerations, he remained rock strong. He maintained the dignity of the office utmost in his approach. This reflected upon the approach of his brother Avtar, too, when he was in similar positions while he served in the Punjab Police. In fact, we all witnessed the respect that Jagjit enjoyed among his peers and subordinates for this.

Jagjit was very particular about his appearance and made it a point to be always smartly turned out. He dressed for the weather and the occasion. He took a lot of pains to ensure that his turban was always perfectly tied. The turban was starched and dried properly to take the correct shape and styled properly. His brother Avtar used to really envy the way Jagjit's turban was always properly tied. When Tej selected an outfit to wear for an occasion, Jagjit made it a point to color-match it with the appropriate turban. He had many neckties and always wore them with a double knot. He taught me the proper method to tie a necktie so that it always came out perfect. This helped me later in life since there were many occasions when I needed to wear a necktie. Jagjit also had a passion for keeping the shine on his shoes. I remember the ritual every weekend when he and us kids used to sit and line up the shoes to polish them for the coming week. He used to insist that we "Blanco" our canvas shoes for school. The procedure entailed the removal of the shoelaces, washing, applying

Blanco (trade name of the popular shoe whitener for canvas shoes) and drying them separately before putting them back once the polish had dried. These small things that we learned from our father remain ingrained in us and we are thankful for it.

Though born a proud practitioner of the Sikh faith, he was open to other faiths. Some of his good friends were of the Muslim and Christian faith. His own daughter-in-law Linda and ex-son-in-law John belonged to the Christian faith. He actively participated in all the festivals and attended Church when invited. He was fully immersed in Canadian traditions and the way of life. His early schooling in the erstwhile undivided India made him fully conversant in Urdu and Persian. He used to make it a point to write to his father in Urdu. When I asked him once about it, since my grandfather corresponded with me in English, Jagjit responded that he and his father both loved Urdu. Jagjit was very fond of Urdu poetry and loved to listen to Ghazals. I never heard him sing, and I doubt he could do so, but I often heard him humming a tune. Jagjit used to attend the gurudwara in Canada whenever he got a chance, though a Tuesday visit was always on the cards. This was so since Tej used to conduct Yoga classes at the Malton Community Center, and the Dixie Gurudwara was enroute. Jagjit was also very particular about grooming his beard. He maintained it to its full length till he breathed his last, even though there were many overtures from the staff caring for him at the long-term care facility to trim it for convenience.

Family time was the greatest joy, and we were imbued with the spirit of loving and giving. Jagjit taught us the value of respect for others by his personal example. He was close to his father-in-law, and I saw it at close quarters that he really meant what he said. He never appeared stressed and believed that a smile could resolve any demanding situation. That approach endeared him to everyone who met him. I do not recollect him losing his temper at anyone or using harsh words. Gentleness was not a sign of weakness, and I know it for certain that he did not accept substandard work from his subordinates. He had such lovely handwriting - he tried his best to get his children to follow him, but I guess he didn't achieve the success he had hoped for. He was very neat and organized. His paperwork and filing were always complete. For him, all things had a place - it reflected less time wasted looking for something out of place.

Our family looked up to him for guidance and support. He was well-read and kept himself up to date with the happenings in the world. It was he who inspired me and my siblings to read the newspaper daily, a practice we cannot do without. Since the early days, he subscribed to Reader's Digest, and he had a collection of Reader's Digest Condensed Books. These volumes had a selection of the finest books, and I, for one, used to read them voraciously. I vividly remember a book called the Reader's Digest Junior Treasury which contained many abridged books and articles that piqued the imagination of a young mind. Some of the contents can be recalled to this day by me, and they bring back pleasant memories. One such story by Jim Corbett on the Maneaters of Kumaon inspired me to take my young family to Corbett National Park to see the tigers in their natural habitat. Moving through the jungle on an elephant was an experience, but alas, we could not witness any tigers as they elected to stay away!

There also was the Readers Digest World Atlas, which had detailed maps. We were encouraged to refer to it to add

Reader's Digest Junior Treasury

to our world knowledge, a habit that formed early on, and it just added to my wanderlust. He took to learning the use of the computer at a later age, but he used to enjoy surfing the net and keeping abreast of the news. He was extremely interested in religion and used to listen to the daily message (*waak*) from the Golden Temple at Amritsar. He was a regular visitor to the gurudwara while in Canada and took the opportunity to visit it when possible. He was very comfortable standing behind the Guru Granth Sahib as a "*sevadar*" (volunteer) and fanning it with the "Chaur Sahib". The Chaur Sahib is made from yak hair, has a wooden handle, and is adorned with some fine carvings. The person fanning the Guru Granth Sahib is paying respect and devotion to the scriptures since they are treated like a living God. The practice of fanning came about from the respect for the rulers and kings of yesteryear.

CHAPTER 14

VISIT TO HEMKUND SAHIB

Jagjit made many visits to India, and it was during one of these in June 1994 that he discussed the idea of a pilgrimage to Hemkund Sahib with Avtar Berar. Avtar was a seasoned visitor to this location and had even walked all the way from Delhi once with a lot of other pilgrims. Avtar had also authored a book on Hemkund containing its historical and religious importance for the Sikhs. Avtar was totally on board with this idea and planned to accompany Jagjit. During discussions, it came about that many other family members also wanted to make the pilgrimage, and eventually Ravinder, Shailly, and Rashmi from Ludhiana were added to the group. Jagjit and Avtar went by road from Delhi to Rishikesh, whereas the group from Ludhiana took the train to Saharanpur and, thereafter, a bus to Rishikesh. They all stayed at the Gurudwara at Rishikesh for the night. The next day, they engaged a taxi and proceeded toward Govindghat. A significant delay was encountered at Joshimath due to traffic restrictions, and the group stayed the night at the Govindghat Gurudwara.

The group was well-prepared, having been properly briefed by Avtar Berar, who was very experienced for this trek. Each person carried their backpack which had a sweater, change of clothes, inners, toiletries, extra bed sheets for hygiene reasons, and raincoats. Though the gurudwara provided basic amenities, the washrooms were clean, and the food was very wholesome. An early departure was made toward Govind Dham and after a trek of about 14 km, they reached the gurudwara in the afternoon. The terrain gradually slopes upwards and there were many people making their way up and returning.

Since Jagjit had a Canadian passport, the group could get a private room in the Gurudwara at Govind Dham. Sufficient mats and bedding were provided. The langar was simple but wholesome. The ladies helped prepare the food, and everyone retired early for an early start the next day for the ascent to Hemkund Sahib.

The climb to the top is very steep, and being situated at about 15,000 ft, there is also a reduction of oxygen, thus making for a slow and gentle ascent. Though only about 6-7 km, the climb takes 5 hours, crossing two small glaciers on the way. These are slippery and treacherous portions, and pitons and ropes are attached to hold on to, for a slip would surely result in some serious problems. It was a welcome sight of the gurudwara beside the Hemkund (Holy Lake), which was surrounded by the seven peaks as described by Guru Gobind Singh in "Vichitra Natak," a rendition of his stay at the location during meditation in an earlier incarnation.

Jagjit at Hemkund Sahib with Shaily and Ravinder

After the mandatory pictures, the group had a quick dip in the freezing waters of the lake. Avtar narrated the whole story of the discovery of the site by some Army personnel many years ago and the whole timeline of the development of the site with the gurudwara, the laying of the path, and other administrative facilities for the pilgrims. Subsequently, after paying due obeisance at the gurudwara, the group began the descent for Govind Dham. This had to be undertaken carefully due to the wet steps and crossing the glaciers. The halt at Govind Dham at the gurudwara was uneventful, and the group benefited from a private room allotted to them again, since Jagjit had a Canadian passport.

The transit from Govind Dham to Govind Ghat was uneventful, but the group was forced to stay the night at the Govind Ghat Gurudwara since their contracted taxi had left and was untraceable. The next day, after connecting with him, the group left for Badrinath. They could not enter the shrine because it was closed for unforeseen reasons. Therefore, they enjoyed the waters of the hot spring to warm up spent time in the local bazaar and enjoyed some hot puris and cholley (chickpeas). The drive to Rishikesh was uneventful, with Ravinder regaling everyone with anecdotes about her siblings. A landslide delayed their arrival at Rishikesh, where they stayed at the gurudwara. The next day, the group split up, with Jagjit and Avtar going back to Delhi and the ladies to Ludhiana by way of Haridwar and Ambala. Jagjit used to fondly reminisce about his wonderful time during this trip, which was quite an adventure in addition to being a pilgrimage.

CHAPTER 15

OTHER INDIA VISITS

Since Jagjit could not get a job in his line in Canada, he could visit India at a time of his choosing. He made it a point to spend time with Sandeep and Linda wherever they were posted, as well as with other relatives in Punjab. He kept up with friends and colleagues and made efforts to familiarize himself with the use of the internet and social media, which were still in their infancy.

Goa Visit 2001

The house at 68 Hargobind Enclave was still in his possession, and he had maintained Nanhi Bai and her family as housekeepers to manage the outdoors. Nanhi Bai was a permanent feature at the house since the construction began, and being very loyal and dependable, it was comfortable leaving the property in their charge. Since Jagjit and Tejwant decided to continue living in Canada, it made a lot of sense to dispose of this property as it was not being used and required maintenance and upkeep. Meanwhile, depending upon availability, they had been living in seniors' subsidized housing in Canada. These frequent moves were an irritant, so they decided to sell the property in Delhi and buy a suitable place in Mississauga. During his visit in 1998, Jagjit made a deal and sold off the house in Hargobind Enclave. After the transfer of funds, he bought a condo on Shipp Drive, which was to be their residence thereafter.

Ancestral Property Consolidation

The ancestral property at Village Bir Puad had been handed down from Jagjit's grandfather. The rules of inheritance prevalent at that time just took the land holdings and divided each field into equal portions among the sons. The daughters had no share of the property since it was assumed that they had been given their share as part of the dowry during their marriage and that she would be part of the family of her husband, who would inherit it from his father. The division of each field posed a logistical challenge since each owner now needed to have independent water channels leading to his portion of the divided field from the existing common well. Further, with shrinking water tables, the availability of water was crucial for the crops and there were frequent disputes regarding the share of the water. Jagjit's father, Hari Singh, had a real brother, Bikram Singh, and therefore, there was a comparable situation of divided fields and a shared well. After the passing of Hari Singh, his holdings were divided among Jagjit and his brother Avtar's widow Amrita. In the case of Bikram Singh, he had only one son, Jasbir Singh, and therefore, all the land holdings got transferred to him as a single unit.

Jagjit realized that this could be consolidated so that each field, which was presently divided, could be reallocated so that it was easier to manage and give out on contract for crop cultivation. He discussed with Jasbir and Amrita and set about getting this done officially. It was a huge administrative task as the boundaries had to be redrawn and revenue books updated with new owner names. Though Jagjit's sister Surinder technically did not have a share of the ancestral property, Jagjit insisted that she be given a third share of the same. Therefore, she was given a cash value of the assessed value of the land holding, and the reallocated lands were registered in the name of the half for Jagjit, and the other half was divided among Amrita and her son, Harbir. The location of the tubewell, which was being shared till now, did not work for the reallocated fields, so Jagjit spent a lot of time getting a new bore for a tubewell made close to the village periphery. The ancestral house had also not been used after the passing away of Jagjit's mother, Beant Kaur, on April 25, 1993, in Chandigarh. Jagjit insisted that the house be handed over to Jasbir and a similar land portion be added to another field during the reallocation. The ancestral house had been constructed with a lot of passion by Jagjit's father and had both sentimental and monetary value as it was built with bricks, unlike many other houses which were mud-based.

This was a monumental task and was only made possible due to Jagjit's sheer perseverance and his spending countless hours working with the bureaucracy. The allocation and installation of the electrical connection, which involved laying down of new lines and many poles, was only made possible due to Jagjit reaching out to some of his connections in the hydel department of which he was part of during his career. The redistribution of the land holdings was key to their disposal after Jagjit had passed and his share passed on to his wife and children. Since all of them resided in Canada, it was a relatively simple sale to do this using a Power of Attorney.

Visit to Rishikesh

Tejwant had taken training at Sheridan College, Oakville, as a qualified Yoga teacher and was also a member of the Federation of Yoga Teachers (FOYT). Once she took retirement from the Allendale facility in Milton, she became a full-time staff at some community centers in Mississauga to conduct Yoga classes. In addition, she conducted Yoga classes in many senior programs as a volunteer. She became involved in the teaching of Pranayama Yoga propagated by Swami Ram Dev. She attended the training courses in Canada for teaching this type of Yoga and Jagjit used to attend them too. He used to affectionately call her "Guruji" for this reason and because she used to care for him.

In 2009, there was a third-level training planned at the Ashram of Swami Ram Dev in Rishikesh. Many other Yoga teachers from Canada had planned to attend this training. Tejwant also wanted to participate, and Jagjit encouraged her and also decided to accompany her. The one-week retreat was beneficial for him as he participated in many activities and treatments. They also became life members of the Patanjali Yog Ashram with an eye for future visits. They also made a trip to the Khajuraho monument complex during this visit. This ancient temple complex in Madhya Pradesh has many intricately carved structures that have stood the test of time.

At Rishikesh

During the return from one of their visits to India, there was a layover in Brussels, Belgium. During that period, Rashmi was living there as her then-husband, Bhavneet, was working on a project. This was a wonderful warm stay with her, and she took them around to the various attractions in and around Brussels. Jagjit and Tej also made a day trip to Paris and did see the major attractions like the Louvre, Champs-Élysées, Arc de Triomphe, and the Eiffel Tower.

Paris – Arc de Triomphe

CHAPTER 16

OTHER TRIPS

Cruises

Jagjit and Tej were quite friendly with Gurdeep and Surinder Dhaliwal. Being close in age and sharing similar interests, they decided to undertake a cruise together. This was to be their first cruise, and they flew to Barcelona for a one-week cruise in the Mediterranean. They visited many ports and really enjoyed the time spent there. For their 50th wedding anniversary, Juhi and John (her husband then) planned a cruise in the Caribbean for a week. Many other family members like Kuku and Guddi, as well as Billoo and Pimmi, accompanied them, and it was a memorable time for everyone.

Golden Anniversary Cruise

Western Canada

Linda's mom, Mabel, was visiting Canada in May 2008. Sandeep and Linda planned a trip to western Canada, and Jagjit and Tej were also on board for this. Consequently, the five of us flew to Calgary on July 27. After renting a car, we dropped in to meet with Gurdev (a cousin of Tej's from her mother Amrit's side) and his family. After a very hospitable lunch, we traveled to Banff. Seeing the Rockies and enjoying the ride up the gondola to the top, we could appreciate the beauty of the area. Walking along the Bow River and admiring the waterfalls made for an unforgettable experience. En route to Jasper, we stopped at Lake Louise and the Columbia Icefields (a glacier). Keeping Jasper as a base, we visited the Athabasca Falls, Maligne Lake, and the other attractions. We next stopped at Kamloops and saw the city attractions. We had picked accommodations at a lovely Bed and Breakfast, and they had the most delicious peaches growing on their property, which we had a chance to enjoy. We spent the next day at White Rock before taking the ferry across to Victoria. This was a wonderful experience to see the marina and the Butchart Gardens. We returned to Vancouver and flew back after dropping off the rental car at the airport. It was a truly memorable trip as we also saw some wildlife, with some elk along the highway.

Lake Louise, AB

Spray Mountain Top, Banff, AB

Eastern Canada

Being members of many senior groups, Jagjit and Tej also participated in many group tours they organized. They went on a five-day trip to the Maritimes with Chitra and Arun Majumdar. This organized tour took them to New Brunswick, Prince Edward Island, and Nova Scotia. It was a great exposure to the Maritimes, and they loved seeing that part of Canada. They also went to Washington and New York on other occasions. They really loved to travel and see various places.

At Golden Temple, Amritsar

CHAPTER 17

Volunteer Activities

Jagjit had volunteered his time to give back to the community. He engaged with the Children's Aid Society in Mississauga and went there regularly. He also was a regular volunteer with the India Rainbow Community Services of Peel (IRCS, now renamed as Indus), a non-profit organization providing services for the South Asian community. Through its many programs, it has a focus on Adult Day Services, Language Instruction, Outreach, and Senior Engagement, among others. Jagjit was a part of the Friendly Visit program which matched a volunteer with a client who was either shut in due to their medical condition or just needed someone to drop by for a conversation and engagement. For this volunteer activity, Jagjit has been recognized many times by the municipal, regional, and provincial authorities and felicitated.

Once Tej took retirement from her job at the Allendale facility in Milton, she started attending the Senior Services program at IRCS along with Jagjit. She also started volunteering by conducting Yoga classes tailored for seniors. They made several friends there and it became a good group when they started having many activities and get-togethers. Arun and Chitra Majumdar; Bob and Uma Talwar; Mohan and Mohini Bharti (both since deceased) were the couples Jagjit and Tej interacted with frequently. Another individual with whom Jagjit became very friendly through his association with IRCS was Denis Jonathan. Denis was originally from Pakistan and had a lengthy career with Air Canada. Jagjit and Denis became close and shared many interests, including going to see movies on Tuesdays when the ticket prices were reduced to half price. Denis stayed close by, and they also went out for walks when the weather was conducive. Denis also offered the use of his Air Canada buddy passes to Jagjit and Tej, which they took advantage of on two occasions – to attend the wedding of Sammy and Sukhdeep (alias Sue) (Billoo and Pimmi's son and daughter-in-law) in San Francisco and then to visit Ashu in Vancouver.

It was the association of Jagjit and Tej with IRCS that I also started volunteering with that organization as a member of the board of Directors. The involvement was very satisfying, and I spent five years on the board, two of which were as the Chair. I was also fortunate to have been involved in the rebranding of this organization to be named as Indus. The organization has grown very well and has a large presence in the community. Indus was also the organization that helped a lot during Jagjit's later years. He was a regular attendee of the Adult Day Program run by this organization.

CHAPTER 18

Jagjit's 80th Birthday Celebrations

We decided to celebrate Jagjit's 80th Birthday in a befitting manner, and the entire family got together in planning for it. The party room of the condo where they lived could accommodate about 35-40 people and was considered adequate to cater for the guest list that included family and friends. Invitations were sent out, and organizational responsibilities were assigned. Food was catered, music was organized, decorations were put up, and some party games were planned. Tania and Pia took it upon themselves to provide a photographic timeline of Jagjit's life. They painstakingly collated old pictures, scanned them, made copies, and put up a display on the walls of the room. Pria made the trip to attend this function specially from Seattle. Almost all of Jagjit's friends attended as well as his entire family. It was a memorable evening, and an enthusiastic bhangra performance was conducted by Jasbir's grandsons (Agamapar and Gurupkar). I had also reached out to the rest of the family and friends who were not local to send personalized messages to Jagjit via a service where they could dial in and record them. These messages were then put onto a CD and presented to Jagjit. He was very touched by this gesture and enjoyed listening to the messages at his own leisure.

Jagjit was also fortunate to have participated in the 75th birthday celebrations of Tejwant, which were done on a grand scale in a Banquet Hall, with over 100 guests attending. He really enjoyed the day standing by her side and delivered a lovely message for her. It is reproduced here:

Good evening, I would like to thank everyone who has made it convenient to be among us to celebrate the 75th Birthday of my dear wife, Tejwant. It is with immense pleasure and joy that I stand beside her in her long journey to this milestone and am thankful to the Almighty that I have been so fortunate to have her as my companion through all these glorious years. I can still vividly remember all the times that we shared - whether they were good or bad - but we came out through them so strong and resilient.

She has been such a source of inspiration and strength that I cannot help but admit that were it not for her tenacity, resourcefulness, and perseverance, I would not be where I am today. She has boundless energy and enthusiasm that are infectious, and she wins over everyone who meets her. She has been so active in the community and has given back so much through her volunteer efforts and Yoga classes while continuing to maintain the obligations of her large immediate and extended family.

I remember the time when we got married and started our small family. Even though she was raising our children, she did so much to bring up my siblings. She had such a great attitude toward my parents and other relatives. We were unfortunate to lose close members of our family at an early age. She was right there to console me and help alleviate the loss. She has worked extremely hard and taken on projects to bring in extra income to offset large expenses. It was only due to her dedication and effort that we managed to get our house in Delhi constructed.

Our move to Canada really brought out her true spirit of independence. She, who had never driven before, was steadfast in her effort to be mobile and rightly achieved her desire. I am so proud to be her spouse and hope that she continues to enjoy good health and happiness. Please join me now as we wish her a Happy Birthday! Thanks.

Tej 75th Birthday Celebrations

CHAPTER 19

Jagjit's Health

Jagjit had been diagnosed with hyperthyroidism earlier, which had been corrected by the administering of radioactive iodine in Delhi, but he still had the symptoms of early diabetes at that time. He took a lot of precautions with his diet and exercised but eventually had to be prescribed medications once he moved to Canada. There was also evidence of higher cholesterol, and despite medication, he had an episode of a partial facial stroke. It was only due to the persistence of Tej that he continued to perform the yogic Pranayam exercises, and this condition was quickly corrected. Since Tej was a trained PSW and had worked with seniors with similar conditions, she could see the symptoms of the onset of Alzheimer's Disease in Jagjit. He started forgetting things, particularly events that related to short-term memory. He would tend to wander off, and this was a matter of concern. Once, during the middle of the night, he opened the door of the condo and wandered out. It could have had serious implications since it was winter, and he was not suitably dressed. This was quickly addressed by installing a lock on the door from the inside.

Tej got him enrolled in the Adult Day Program with IRCS (now renamed as Indus), the same organization where he had volunteered in the past. They had a wonderful program for seniors in a similar situation as Jagjit, and they kept them for the entire day and provided meals. Mental aerobics and other board games were conducted to keep their faculties active. This also provided Tej a break from looking after Jagjit full-time and pursuing her own volunteering activities. Since Jagjit's kids lived nearby, they also dropped in frequently to check in and provide support. There was also in-home care provided by the medical authorities where a worker used to come home and provide a shower and dressing facility for Jagjit. Despite the quality care and comfort provided to him, it soon became apparent that Jagjit needed 24/7 professional care.

An application was made for admission to a long-term care facility, and an assessment was conducted by the authorities for this. Jagjit was admitted to a facility that had a floor exclusively for patients with dementia so that appropriate trained staff was made available for their care. Jagjit adapted well and had regular visits from Tej, his kids, and other family members. Slowly, his condition kept deteriorating, and he could only recognize his near ones. His weight kept dropping as his appetite reduced. Toward the end of 2014, he stopped eating, and the staff advised that only comfort should be provided. Jagjit breathed his last in the early morning on Jan 10, 2015.

Prior arrangements had been made for this eventuality, and the mortal remains were kept at the Meadowvale Visitation Center in Brampton. A viewing was conducted the next evening, followed by the cremation at the same location on Jan 12, 2015. This was followed by a prayer service at the Dixie Gurudwara in Brampton. There was a large turnout of family and friends for these events. Numerous others called and sent their condolences. There was an obituary in the Toronto Star newspaper, and many local language newspapers carried a small write-up about Jagjit in their editions.

JAGJIT ATWAL

JAGJIT ATWAL It is with great sadness that we announce the passing away of Jagjit in his 86th year on January 10, 2015. Jagjit leaves behind his beloved wife Tejwant, children Sandeep (Linda), Manoj (Harbir) and Juhi Kaunds (John) and nephew Sukhjit (Mandeep) and grandchildren Tania, Ambika, Pia, Samay, Amol and Udai. Family and friends will be received at Meadowvale Visitation Centre, 7732 Mavis Road, Brampton, ON, L6Y 5L5, from 6 to 8 p.m. on Sunday, January 11, 2015. Funeral services will be held at the same location on Monday, January 12, 2015 from 12:00 to 2:30 p.m., followed by a prayer service at the Dixie Gurudwara, 7080 Dixie Road, Mississauga, ON, L5S 1B7. Donations in lieu of flowers should be made toward India Rainbow Community Services of Peel at 905-275-2369 or www.indiarainbow.org

Jagjit Obituary

CHAPTER 20

Epilogue

Significance of Gurudwara Patal Puri

Gurudwara Patal Puri is where Sri Guru Hargobind Sahib Ji, Sri Guru Har Rai Ji, and the mother of Sri Guru Tegh Bahadur Ji, Mata Nanaki, were cremated. Their ashes were dispersed into the river, as was the case of Sri Guru Har Krishan Ji.

The place where the Gurudwara Charan Kanwal is today used to be the home of a pandit named Peenju. He had heard from the villagers and travelers that there was a Pir by the name of Nanak who gave sight to the blind and speech to the dumb. In his heart, the pandit had adopted Sri Guru Nanak Dev Ji as his Guru and had practiced prema-bhakti for his darshan.

During their travels, Guru Nanak had come upon the home of Peenju and had blessed their bhagat. At that very spot, Guru Nanak had begun kirtan with Mardana and had remained immersed in it for three hours until Mardana had stopped playing his rabab, which caused Guru Nanak to open his lotus eyes and question Mardana as to why he had stopped. Mardana said, "Either make me as thyself or at least ask if I am hungry once in a while." Guru Nanak Ji was pleased with his innocent answer and had blessed him with the sound of the unstruck melodies. After Mardana had remained immersed in the anhad shabad for hours, Guru Ji laid their hand on top of Mardana's head and brought his consciousness back to its normality. Mardana had praised his Guru and had tried to explain the overflow of bliss he had experienced.

Mardana had then asked Guru Ji the significance of this land as he had experienced such celestial fortune upon it. Guru Nanak, being pleased with his question, had said that "You are my *sevak* and I will not hide anything from you." Sri Guru Nanak Dev Ji went on to explain that "In the coming years when I assume my 6th avatar, I will construct this land and name it Kiratpur. This place had been an oasis of penance in Satjug where many Rishis and Munis had meditated. Also, underneath this sacred land flows the Ganges waters of the netherworld." Guru Ji went on saying, "Vashisht, the master of Ramchander, had spent many years meditating here, and the kingdom of Bali, the Charitable King from Satjug, was also located at this very spot." Upon hearing this, Mardana was in wonderment and had praised his Guru.

Sant Darbara Singh Ji of Lopon constructed the Gurudwara Patal Puri. When Sant Ji returned to India from England, many English folks were intrigued by his discourse on Sri Guru Granth Sahib Ji and decided to come with him and witness the sacred temples and Gurudwaras. Upon reaching Kiratpur Sahib, the English folk were told of the significance of Kiratpur, how ashes of the deceased are poured into the river, but the English were astonished at the fact that such a holy place had not been constructed and why it existed amidst jungle and forest. After hearing the disappointment in their voices, Sant Ji witnessed the parthak darshan of Sri Guru Hargobind Sahib Ji. Understanding this vision as a sign to commence construction of the Gurudwara, Sant Ji announced the plans to construct Gurudwara Patal Puri to the Sangat in Ludhiana on the 18th of May 1976. This gurudwara was then constructed and was given to the sangat and the S.G.P.C. upon completion.

Jagjit's Ashes Immersion

It was Jagjit's wish to have his ashes immersed in the traditional manner at Gurudwara Patalpuri at Kiratpur Sahib in Punjab. Accordingly, after collecting the urn containing his ashes from the crematorium, we started planning the execution of his wishes. Clearance was needed from the Indian High Commission in Toronto to take them along by air to India. After completing the formalities, I accompanied my mother, Tej, to Chandigarh in February 2015, where we stayed with Amrita. Her son, Harbir had planned for transportation to Kiratpur Sahib and arranged for a priest to conduct a small ceremony for the immersion. There are very good arrangements made for conducting this ceremony and a small channel has been diverted from the Beas River where one can do the final ceremony. We were a small group, and the priest was very efficient and conducted the ceremony with prayers. He then instructed me to open the urn containing the ashes of my father and slowly immerse them into the waters. As I did so, I was overcome with emotions that this act symbolized the final act of saying goodbye to his mortal remains. Even so, I felt that this was quite befitting, since Jagjit had worked his professional career among the hydel projects in the area, and his ashes were being immersed in the waters of the River Beas.

Family Tree

Jagjit Side
Beant Atwal
Hari Atwal
Tejwant Atwal
Jagjit Atwal
Jagjit Bhullar
Surinder Dhillon
Rajbir Dhillon
Amrita Atwal
Arter Atwal
Linda Atwal
Sandeep Atwal
Harbir Atwal
Manoj Atwal
Juhi Atwal
Gurpreet Bhullar
Mandeep Bhullar
Sukhjit Bhullar
Duplicate: Gurpreet Bhullar
Pria Sarai
Kuljinder Sarai
Navraj Dhillon
Ruth Dhillon
Savraj Dhillon
Aman Atwal
Harbir Atwal
Pia Atwal-Gooding
Clarence Gooding
Amaryllis Jones
Samay Atwal
Ambika Atwal
Bobby
Tania Chahal
Amol Bhullar
Udai Bhullar
Sonia Sarai
Sareena Sarai
Raveena Sarai
Sumer Atwal
Mark Gooding
Oliver Gooding
Serena Jones-Atwal
Rudra

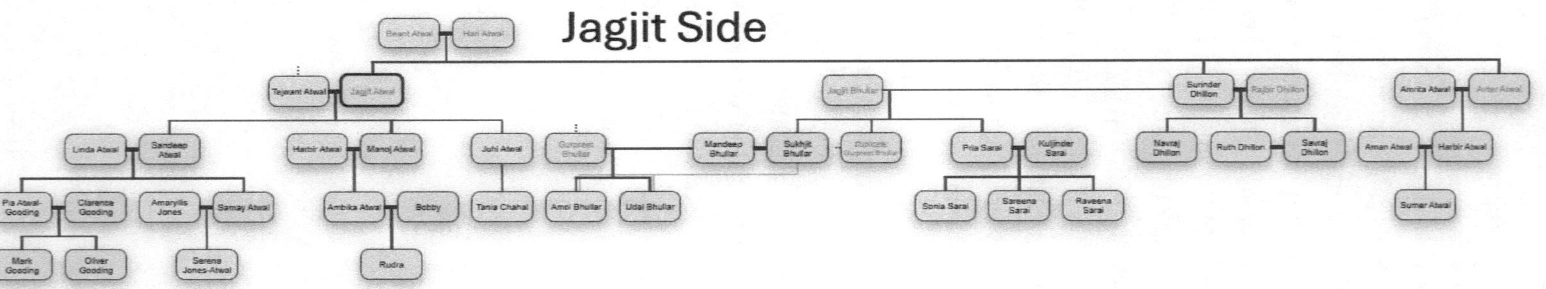

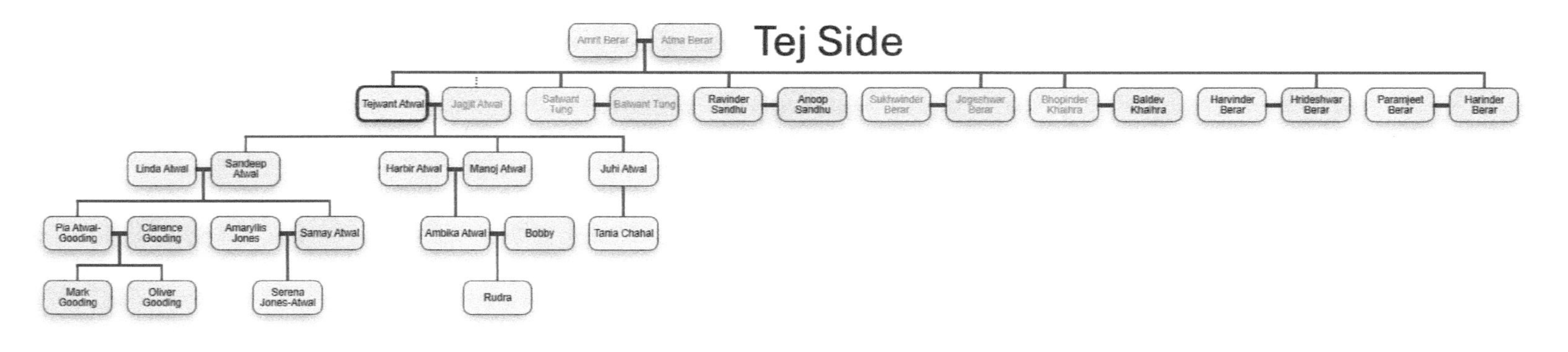

Tej Side
Amrit Berar
Atma Berar
Tejwant Atwal
Jagjit Atwal
Satwant Tung
Balwant Tung
Ravinder Sandhu
Anoop Sandhu
Sukhwinder Berar
Jogeshwar Berar
Bhopinder Khaihra
Baldev Khaihra
Harvinder Berar
Hrideshwar Berar
Paramjeet Berar
Harinder Berar
Linda Atwal
Sandeep Atwal
Harbir Atwal
Manoj Atwal
Juhi Atwal
Pia Atwal-Gooding
Clarence Gooding
Amaryllis Jones
Samay Atwal
Ambika Atwal
Bobby
Tania Chahal
Mark Gooding
Oliver Gooding
Serena Jones-Atwal
Rudra